MW01173306

CLASSICAL CHRISTIAN VIRTUES

Contemplating the Good Life

DR. TIMOTHY DERNLAN

Titus Books
Philadelphia, PA

Titus Books

Classical Christian Virtues:
Contemplating the Good Life

Version 2.1

© 2020 by Timothy Dernlan

ISBN: 979-8-61150-074-3

Contact Information:
Dr. Timothy Dernlan
www.timdernlan.com

1. Christian Virtues   2. Virtue Ethics   3. Spiritual Formation

First Edition: January 2020

Printed in the United States of America

To those who have been knocked down
by the difficulties of life in a fallen world.

May you abide in Christ.

Table of Contents

CHAPTER I

CHAPTER II

CHAPTER III

REFERENCES

ABOUT THE AUTHOR

8

CHAPTER I

Introduction

Whether we are young or old, experienced or inexperienced, immature or mature, we are often faced with difficult decisions. When faced with hard choices, we often ask ourselves and others, "What should I do?" Aristotle suggested that this is the wrong question. Instead, he advocated that we ask, "What kind of person do I want to be?" This is the guiding question and reoccurring focus of this book.

So, what kind of person do you want to be? Hopefully, you are already a Christian, and you want to be like Jesus. You were created *imago dei* – in the image of God – and as a Christian, you have the Holy Spirit living inside you. That is amazing and should be a great encouragement to you! Being made in God's image, having Jesus as your living example, and with the power of the Holy Spirit to guide you, you can become a more virtuous and Christ-like person.

This book is a practical guide for understanding virtue formation and personal development in virtues. As you go through this study, you might be surprised at some of the virtues that made the list. First, contemplate each virtue on a macro-theoretical level and also on a micro-practical level. Next, think about the ways you have seen the virtue displayed in the lives of others from the Bible, history, literature, and film. Then, take time to contemplate each virtue and vice as they are exhibited in your own life. Finally, find ways to apply each one practically to your life, and seek specific ways to improve and move toward a more virtuous life.

The table of virtues (listed at the end of this chapter) will serve as the road map of this study. It is inspired by Aristotle's "golden mean." Aristotle believed a virtue is found at the midpoint (the "golden mean") between excess (too much of a good thing) and deficiency (too little of a good thing). This is good guidance; however, please remember not to rely on the ancients for your final authority as you (or your study group) contemplate what it means to be virtuous. Instead, remind yourself and encourage the individuals in your group to look to the Ancient of Days for the final word of truth.

The table of virtues and questions throughout the book will help guide your discussions as you train yourself (or your students) to be more virtuous citizens. Remember, we are citizens of our family, teams, clubs, schools, tribes, local community, state, country, and, most importantly, citizens of the kingdom of Christ.

At this point, you might be excited to begin this journey toward becoming more virtuous. Your excitement might tempt you to rush through this book like a rock skipping over a pond. If this describes you, please resist this temptation. Take enough time to ponder and contemplate each virtue. Let yourself or your study group meander through each discussion like a winding country stream.

The process of questioning and contemplation as you discuss the following topics will allow the golden mean of each virtue to be planted in the most fertile soil deep within you - so that each virtue might grow strong in your life and provide cool water and a restful shade for you and others who encounter you.

Small Groups

This book is formatted to be most effectively used in a group setting. I would like to strongly encourage you to form a "Classical Christian Virtues Group" to discuss the virtues and vices presented in this book. Taking time to form a group and contemplate "the good life" together with trusted friends will not only deepen your relationships with your life's traveling companions, but it will also more deeply develop your commitment to becoming a more virtuous person through verbalizing the areas on which you will focus your development.

Leaders of a "Classical Christian Virtues Group" should not stand and present in a lecture-style format. Instead, sit in a circle with your group, and be a participant mentor and guide. You might want to have refreshments while you talk. Feel free to walk through nature or a neighborhood as you talk about the virtues. If you would rather sit to talk, consider gathering in an outdoor space or a beautiful room rather than in a classroom with rows of desks. If a classroom is your only option, arrange the desks or chairs into a circle to create a more relaxed and engaging environment. Encourage members of your group to write notes and ideas in this book or to use a commonplace book to record their thoughts and ideas during the discussion.

Finally, lead with questions to solicit participation before almost every quote, statement, definition, verse of Scripture, or statement presented to you in the following pages. Seek to lead yourself and your group to new discoveries rather than simply presenting information. By following this format, you might be surprised at the many great stories, examples, and ideas that are generated. Allow yourself and the group to linger on the more interesting and thought-provoking ideas that seem to awaken curiosity and moral imagination.

Individuals

If you are not able (or ready) to contemplate and cultivate virtues with other individuals in your life, you might choose to use this book for personal development on your own. This private contemplation can be a special time of growth and formation toward becoming a more fully formed person. Cultivating virtues through self-examination is a very important part of achieving "the good life" but can sometimes lead to a wide range of emotions as you uncover previously unknown blind spots and weaknesses in your life.

You might need one day, one month, or one year to meditate on just one virtue. Allow yourself time to contemplate, explore, or research the quotes, verses, and ideas in this book rather than racing through each section. Then, seek to change your thoughts and actions as you encounter opportunities to be more virtuous each day. Becoming a person of virtue takes time, effort, and patience.

Table of Virtues

The following table of virtues can be used for quick reference as you contemplate virtue each day or during times that you are struggling with a difficult decision. This is not an exhaustive list of virtues but rather a starting point from which you can explore and enjoy cultivating virtue for the rest of your life. You should also take time to contemplate how each "vice of excess" and "vice of deficiency" flows from a deformed virtue. Feel free to develop your own ideas for virtues to be added to this list or vices of deficiency or excess that may fit better with each virtue.

(-) in deficiency	VIRTUE	(+) in excess
rigidness	**Adaptation**	doublemindedness
timidity	**Bravery**	recklessness
anxiety	**Calmness**	inactivity
cruelty	**Compassion**	permissiveness
irritability	**Contentment**	slothfulness
disagreeableness	**Cooperation**	groupthink
cowardice	**Courage**	impulsiveness
indifference	**Curiosity**	meddling
fickleness	**Dedication**	mania
unreliability	**Dependability**	stubbornness
debasement	**Dignity**	gloating
laziness	**Diligence**	workaholism
hardheartedness	**Empathy**	enablement
apathy	**Endurance**	obstinacy
skepticism	**Faithfulness***	ruthlessness
rudeness	**Friendliness**	flattery
legalism	**Forgiveness**	leniency
hastiness	**Foresight**	indecisiveness
timidity	**Fortitude**	obstinacy
stinginess	**Generosity**	extravagance
anger	**Gentleness***	detachment
evilness	**Goodness***	perfectionism
crudeness	**Grace**	indulgence
churlishness	**Gratitude**	groveling
deceitfulness	**Honesty**	outspokenness
negligence	**Honor**	controlling
pessimism	**Hope**	naivety
aloofness	**Hospitality**	stifling
pride	**Humility**	degradation
laziness	**Industriousness**	workaholism
corruption	**Integrity**	legalism
apathy	**Joy***	flamboyance
corruption	**Justice**	detachment

13

(-) in deficiency	VIRTUE	(+) in excess
hostility	**Kindness***	foolishness
selfishness	**Love***	permissiveness
treachery	**Loyalty**	thoughtlessness
arrogance	**Meekness**	timidity
cruelty	**Mercy**	shamefulness
shamelessness	**Modesty**	shyness
rebellion	**Obedience**	passiveness
anxiety	**Optimism**	naivety
confusion	**Orderliness**	nagging
restlessness	**Patience***	laziness
anxiety	**Peace***	impotence
negligence	**Pensiveness**	criticalness
passiveness	**Perseverance**	arrogance
apathy	**Purposefulness**	worry
disregard	**Respect**	idolatry
unreliability	**Responsibility**	workaholism
wastefulness	**Resourcefulness**	stinginess
irreverence	**Righteousness**	haughtiness
wildness	**Self-Control***	stoicism
unfeeling	**Sensitivity**	anxiety
inconsideration	**Servanthood**	slavery
stubbornness	**Teachability**	naivety
carelessness	**Thoughtfulness**	withdrawn
prejudice	**Tolerance**	licentiousness
deception	**Truthfulness**	rudeness
ignorance	**Wisdom**	disdain
boorishness	**Wit**	buffoonery

* In Galatians 5:22-23, Paul teaches us that Christians should express certain virtues without reservation or limitation. When contemplating these virtues, be sure to read these verses and consider the idea that there is "no law" against the

virtuous characteristics that are a product of the Holy Spirit living inside of us.

But the fruit of the Spirit is
love, joy, peace, patience, kindness,
goodness, faithfulness, gentleness, self-control;
against such things there is no law.
Galatians 5:22-23

Using this Book

There are several approaches you can use to contemplate the virtues presented in this book. You can read from front to back, for specific needs, or as a reference book.

Front to Back
Reading this book from front to back will open you up to surprising new discoveries of unexpected growth. Understanding that you might have blind spots in your life allows you to grow in new ways. Reading this book of virtues from front to back can add a necessary element of surprise and joyful discovery.

Specific Need
Targeting areas of specific need, improvement, and growth in your life will allow you to use this book as a valuable resource to help cultivate specific virtues. This personalized application is well suited for individuals seeking to target specific virtues.

Reference Book
Cultivating virtues, values, and spiritual formation is a daily part of the human experience. This book can be used as a reference guide for Bible verses or recalibration of thoughts

and actions. Keeping this book on your coffee table or an easily accusable bookshelf allow you to quickly pop it open to a virtue that comes to mind as you talk with a spouse, friend, child, or as you individually read and contemplate the virtues presented in great books.

Conclusion

Cultivating virtues ultimately leads us to a deeper appreciation and love for the only truly virtuous one, our Savior Jesus Christ. I pray that this study will help set the table for you to interact with the Holy Spirit to discover more about yourself, our triune God, and others.

Whether you are using this guidebook in a classroom, Bible study, small group, family devotion, or individually, start each of your readings with prayer, and let the Holy Spirit guide your curiosity and desire to become more virtuous as you think, believe, and act on what you discover.

CHAPTER II

Cultivating Virtue

Before continuing to the focus of this study, take time to prepare your heart, mind, and body to gain new wisdom that will influence your actions. Your actions, in turn, determine your level of virtue or vice in a particular area of your life. After contemplating a virtue, make prayerful and intentional choices to improve your level of virtue by taking new action in small ways each day in your life. This will help you to become a person of virtue.

You will gain the most benefit from the following guided contemplations by focusing on each quotation, definition, Scripture, and question. Pondering each section and making yourself physically write a response to the questions in the spaces or margins provided will help to clarify your reasoning and assumptions in your life. Clarifying your own mental models and habits will reveal areas of potential personal growth.

Finally, seek to understand why the author chose each vice of excess or vice of deficiency. Some of them might not be easily understood and seem unrelated; however, taking time to seek the connections will help you dig into a wider range of emotions, life experiences, and empathic understanding. Then, seek to "argue" with the author or debate with your virtue group to develop your own vices related to the virtue you are studying. This will help you uncover deeper areas of virtue and vice as you seek a Christlike life of virtue.

Cultivating Virtue

Contemplation #1

(-) in deficiency	**VIRTUE**	(+) in excess
rigidness	**Adaptation**	doublemindedness

"The measure of intelligence is the ability to change."
Albert Einstein

ADAPTATION

Definition: change or the process of change by which a person becomes better suited to a situation or environment

In Luke 5:17-39, we read about Jesus adapting what He was doing to help a man who was lowered down through a roof in front of Him while He was teaching. He did not send the man and his friends away. Instead, He adapted to the need in front of Him, healed the man, and used the situation to complement what He was already doing.

On one of those days, as he was teaching, Pharisees and teachers of the law were sitting there, who had come from every village of Galilee and Judea and from Jerusalem. And the power of the Lord was with him to heal. And behold, some men were bringing on a bed a man who was paralyzed, and they were seeking to bring him in and lay him before Jesus, but finding no way to bring him in, because of the crowd, they went up on the roof and let him down with his bed through the tiles into the midst before Jesus. And when he saw their faith, he said, "Man, your sins are forgiven you." And the scribes and the Pharisees began to question, saying, "Who is this who speaks blasphemies? Who can forgive sins but God alone?" When

19

Jesus perceived their thoughts, he answered them, "Why do you question in your hearts? Which is easier, to say, 'Your sins are forgiven you,' or to say, 'Rise and walk'? But that you may know that the Son of Man has authority on earth to forgive sins" - he said to the man who was paralyzed - "I say to you, rise, pick up your bed and go home." And immediately he rose up before them and picked up what he had been lying on and went home, glorifying God. And amazement seized them all, and they glorified God and were filled with awe, saying, "We have seen extraordinary things today."
Luke 5:17-39

Guiding Questions

What person in the Bible, history, literature, or film needed to adapt?

When, why, and how should we (or should we NOT) adapt to new ideas, circumstances, or surroundings?

Vices

Adaptation can be a virtue in its best and most pure form, but it can quickly become a vice in its extreme form (doublemindedness) or when it is lacking (rigidness). Continue contemplating adaptation by looking at these two misrepresentations of this virtue.

(+) Doublemindedness

Definition: wavering in thought to the point of indecision and appearing to be two-faced or spineless

A double-minded person is unstable in all his ways.
James 1:8

(-) Rigidness

Definition: unable to change or consider new ways to interact with people or tasks

Now as they went on their way, Jesus entered a village. And a woman named Martha welcomed him into her house. And she had a sister called Mary, who sat at the Lord's feet and listened to his teaching. But Martha was distracted with much serving. And she went up to him and said, "Lord, do you not care that my sister has left me to serve alone? Tell her then to help me." But the Lord answered her, "Martha, Martha, you are anxious and troubled about many things, but one thing is necessary. Mary has chosen the good portion, which will not be taken away from her."
Luke 10:38-42

Guiding Questions

When have you experienced a person being doubleminded or rigid?

What situations cause you to be doubleminded or rigid?

When have you experienced adaptation from someone in your life?

How can you cultivate the virtue of adaptation in your life?

Circle a number to rate yourself in this virtue:

(-) rigidness			**Adaptation**	doublemindedness (+)		
1	2	3	4	5	4	3	2	1

What kind of person do you want to be?

I am doubleminded when...

I am rigid when...

I am adaptable when...

I want to be...

Cultivating Virtue

Contemplation #2

(-) in deficiency	**VIRTUE**	(+) in excess
timidity	**Bravery**	recklessness

"We become brave by doing brave acts."
Aristotle

BRAVERY

Definition: the quality or state of having or showing mental or moral strength to face danger, fear, or difficulty

In I Samuel 17, we read about the bravery of young David as he faced the mighty warrior Goliath. What a wonderful example of actions perfectly balanced between recklessness and timidity. The following passage of Scripture reveals that David had become brave by doing brave acts when he was by himself with nobody watching. So, when it came time for a public act of bravery, it appeared "easy" for David to continue the life of bravery that he had already developed.

And David said to Saul, "Let no man's heart fail because of him. Your servant will go and fight with this Philistine." And Saul said to David, "You are not able to go against this Philistine to fight with him, for you are but a youth, and he has been a man of war from his youth." But David said to Saul, "Your servant used to keep sheep for his father. And when there came a lion, or a bear, and took a lamb from the flock, I went after him and struck him and delivered it out of his mouth. And if he arose against me, I caught him by his beard and struck him and killed him. Your servant has struck down both lions and bears, and this uncircumcised

23

Philistine shall be like one of them, for he has defied the armies of the living God." And David said, "The Lord who delivered me from the paw of the lion and from the paw of the bear will deliver me from the hand of this Philistine." And Saul said to David, "Go, and the Lord be with you!"
I Samuel 17:32-37

Guiding Questions

What person in the Bible, history, literature, or film needed to be brave?

When, why, and how should we be brave when confronted with new ideas, circumstances, or surroundings?

Vices
Bravery can be a virtue in its best and most pure form, but it can quickly become a vice in its extreme form (recklessness) or when it is lacking (timidity). Continue contemplating bravery by looking at these two misrepresentations of this virtue.

(+) Recklessness
Definition: lack of regard for the danger or consequences of one's actions

One who is wise is cautious and turns away from evil, but a fool is reckless and careless.
Proverbs 14:16

(-) Timidity
Definition: lack of proper courage or confidence

For God gave us a spirit not of fear but of power and love and self-control. Therefore, do not be ashamed of the

24

testimony about our Lord, nor of me his prisoner, but share in suffering for the gospel by the power of God.
2 Timothy 1:7-8

Guiding Questions

When have you experienced a person being reckless or timid?

What situations cause you to be reckless or timid?

When have you experienced bravery from someone in your life?

When can you cultivate the virtue of bravery in your life?

Circle a number to rate yourself in this virtue:

(-) timidity			**Bravery**			recklessness (+)		
1	2	3	4	5	4	3	2	1

What kind of person do you want to be?

I am reckless when...

I am timid when...

I am brave when...

I want to be...

Cultivating Virtue

Contemplation #3

(-) in deficiency	**VIRTUE**	(+) in excess
anxiety	**Calmness**	inactivity

"The true strength of a man is in calmness."
Leo Tolstoy

CALMNESS

Definition: a state of tranquility or peace; typically, free from agitation, excitement, or anxiety

Sheep are nervous creatures. They are easily scared and need a great deal of guidance and supervision. If they lose their way and wander from the flock, they will often struggle to find their way back home. David, the author of the book of Psalms, was a great shepherd and knew about the similarities between sheep and people from firsthand experience. In Psalm 23, he reminds us that we can have a calm confidence in the perfect Great Shepherd who will always provide for our every need.

The Lord is my shepherd; I shall not want. He makes me lie down in green pastures. He leads me beside still waters. He restores my soul. He leads me in paths of righteousness for his name's sake. Even though I walk through the valley of the shadow of death, I will fear no evil, for you are with me; your rod and your staff, they comfort me. You prepare a table before me in the presence of my enemies; you anoint my head with oil; my cup overflows. Surely goodness and mercy shall follow me all the days of my life, and I shall dwell in the house of the Lord forever.
Psalm 23:1-6

Guiding Questions

What person in the Bible, history, literature, or film exhibited calmness?

When, why, and how should we (or should we NOT) be calm when facing new ideas, circumstances, or surroundings?

Vices

Calmness can be a virtue in its best and most pure form, but it can quickly become a vice in its extreme form (inactivity) or when it is lacking (anxiety). Continue contemplating calm by looking at these two misrepresentations of this virtue.

(+) Inactivity

Definition: not engaging in or involving any or much physical movement or action

He who observes the wind will not sow, and he who regards the clouds will not reap. As you do not know the way the spirit comes to the bones in the womb of a woman with child, so you do not know the work of God who makes everything. In the morning sow your seed, and at evening withhold not your hand, for you do not know which will prosper, this or that, or whether both alike will be good.
Ecclesiastes 11:4-6

(-) Anxiety

Definition: a feeling of worry, nervousness, or unease, typically about an imminent event or something with an uncertain outcome

Do not be anxious about anything, but in everything by prayer and supplication with thanksgiving let your requests be made known to God. And the peace of God, which

surpasses all understanding, will guard your hearts and your minds in Christ Jesus.
Philippians 4:6-7

Guiding Questions

When have you experienced a person being inactive or anxious?

What situations cause you to be inactive or anxious?

When have you experienced calmness from someone in your life?

How can you cultivate the virtue of calmness in your life?

Circle a number to rate yourself in this virtue:

(-) anxiety			Calmness			inactivity (+)		
1	2	3	4	5	4	3	2	1

What kind of person do you want to be?

I am inactive when...

I am anxious when...

I am calm when...

I want to be...

Cultivating Virtue

Contemplation #4

(-) in deficiency	**VIRTUE**	(+) in excess
cruelty	**Compassion**	permissiveness

*"There never was any heart truly great and generous,
that was not also tender and compassionate."*
Robert Frost

COMPASSION

Definition: sympathetic awareness of the distress of others coupled with a desire to alleviate the pain or discomfort being caused

Have you ever seen someone who needed your help and then chosen to look the other way and do nothing to help them? You may have justified your lack of compassion in many ways. However, the following passage of Scripture is a convicting reminder that we should seek a life of compassion toward others even if it takes you into dangerous circumstances or uncomfortable surroundings.

Jesus replied, "A man was going down from Jerusalem to Jericho, and he fell among robbers, who stripped him and beat him and departed, leaving him half dead. Now by chance a priest was going down that road, and when he saw him he passed by on the other side. So likewise a Levite, when he came to the place and saw him, passed by on the other side. But a Samaritan, as he journeyed, came to where he was, and when he saw him, he had compassion. He went to him and bound up his wounds, pouring on oil and wine. Then he set him on his own animal and brought him to an

31

inn and took care of him. And the next day he took out two denarii and gave them to the innkeeper, saying, 'Take care of him, and whatever more you spend, I will repay you when I come back."
Luke 10:30-35

Guiding Questions

What person in the Bible, history, literature, or film needed compassion?

When, why, and how should we (or should we NOT) be compassionate to new ideas, circumstances, or surroundings?

Vices

Compassion can be a virtue in its best and most pure form, but it can quickly become a vice in its extreme form (permissiveness) or when it is lacking (cruelty). Continue contemplating compassion by looking at these two misrepresentations of this virtue.

(+) Permissiveness

Definition: allowing excessive freedom of behavior beyond what is good

Whoever loves discipline loves knowledge, but he who hates correction is stupid.
Proverbs 12:1

(-) Cruelty

Definition: callous indifference to or pleasure in causing pain and suffering

Whoever oppresses a poor man insults his Maker, but he who is generous to the needy honors him.
Proverbs 14:31

Guiding Questions

When have you experienced a person being permissive or cruel?

What situations cause you to be permissive or cruel?

When have you experienced compassion from someone in your life?

How can you cultivate the virtue of compassion in your life?

Circle a number to rate yourself in this virtue:

(-) cruelty			**Compassion**		permissiveness (+)		
1	2	3	4	5	4	3	2	1

What kind of person do you want to be?

I am permissive when...

I am cruel when...

I am compassionate when...

I want to be...

Cultivating Virtue

Contemplation #5

(-) in deficiency	**VIRTUE**	(+) in excess
irritability	**Contentment**	slothfulness

"The greatest wealth is to live content with little."
Plato

CONTENTMENT

Definition: the quality of being satisfied with the current state of life events, circumstances, and interpersonal relationships

Contentment has been a struggle throughout all of history. From the moment of creation, humanity was not content. Adam and Eve were given a beautiful paradise for a home, fulfilling work, and a face-to-face relationship with God himself. However, Satan used the vice of discontentment to tempt our first parents into a sin the world will suffer with until all things are made new, and we return to paradise. Paul addresses the virtue of contentment and reminds the Philippians not to rely on other people or circumstances for their contentment. Our ultimate contentment can only be found through the strength of Christ alone when we humbly submit every small and major concern to Him.

I rejoiced in the Lord greatly that now at length you have revived your concern for me. You were indeed concerned for me, but you had no opportunity. Not that I am speaking of being in need, for I have learned in whatever situation I am to be content. I know how to be brought low, and I know how to abound. In any and every circumstance, I have learned the secret of facing plenty and hunger, abundance

and need. I can do all things through him who strengthens me.
Philippians 4:10-13

Guiding Questions

What person in the Bible, history, literature, or film needed contentment?

When, why, and how should we (or should we NOT) be content with new ideas, circumstances, or surroundings?

Vices
Contentment can be a virtue in its best and most pure form, but it can quickly become a vice in its extreme form (slothfulness) or when it is lacking (irritability). Continue contemplating contentment by looking at these two misrepresentations of this virtue.

(+) Slothfulness
Definition: laziness or reluctance to work, make an effort, or improve

Through sloth the roof sinks in, and through indolence the house leaks.
Ecclesiastes 10:18

(-) Irritability
Definition: having or showing a tendency to be easily annoyed or made angry

A fool gives full vent to his spirit, but a wise man quietly holds it back.
Proverbs 29:11

Guiding Questions

When have you experienced a person being slothful or irritable?

What situations cause you to be slothful or irritable?

When have you experienced contentment from someone in your life?

How can you cultivate the virtue of contentment in your life?

Circle a number to rate yourself in this virtue:

(-) irritability			Contentment		slothfulness (+)		
1	2	3	4	5	4	3	2	1

What kind of person do you want to be?

I am slothful when...

I am irritable when...

I am content when...

I want to be...

Cultivating Virtue

Contemplation #6

(-) in deficiency	**VIRTUE**	(+) in excess
disagreeableness	**Cooperation**	groupthink

"Coming together is a beginning,
staying together is progress,
and working together is success."
Henry Ford

COOPERATION

Definition: the process of working together to achieve the same goal or accomplish a common task

In Philippians 2:1-4, Paul encourages believers to be united in Christian community and cooperation as they live together. Cooperation requires humility and an understanding that there is a greater good that unites us to a common purpose. Cooperation toward a true, good, and beautiful goal allows us to glorify God as a body of believers.

So, if there is any encouragement in Christ, any comfort from love, any participation in the Spirit, any affection and sympathy, complete my joy by being of the same mind, having the same love, being in full accord and of one mind. Do nothing from selfish ambition or conceit, but in humility count others more significant than yourselves. Let each of you look not only to his own interests, but also to the interests of others.
Philippians 2:1-4

Guiding Questions

What person in the Bible, history, literature, or film needed to cooperate?

When, why, and how should we (or should we NOT) cooperate with coworkers, parents, siblings, teachers, and/or classmates?

Vices

Cooperation can be a virtue in its best and most pure form, but it can quickly become a vice in its extreme form (groupthink) or when it is lacking (disagreeableness). Continue contemplating cooperation by looking at these two misrepresentations of this virtue.

(+) Groupthink

Definition: the practice of thinking or making decisions as a group in a way that discourages creativity or individual responsibility

You shall not fall in with the many to do evil, nor shall you bear witness in a lawsuit, siding with the many, so as to pervert justice.
Exodus 23:2

(-) Disagreeableness

Definition: unfriendly and bad tempered in a way that makes things needlessly difficult

He who is often reproved, yet stiffens his neck, will suddenly be broken beyond healing.
Proverbs 29:1

Guiding Questions

When have you experienced groupthink or disagreeableness?

What situations cause you to follow groupthink or be disagreeable?

When have you experienced cooperation from someone in your life?

How can you cultivate the virtue of cooperation in your life?

Circle a number to rate yourself in this virtue:

(-) disagreeableness	Cooperation	groupthink (+)

| 1 | 2 | 3 | 4 | 5 | 4 | 3 | 2 | 1 |

What kind of person do you want to be?

I fall into groupthink when...

I am disagreeable when...

I am cooperative when...

I want to be...

Cultivating Virtue

Contemplation #7

(-) in deficiency	**VIRTUE**	(+) in excess
cowardice	**Courage**	impulsiveness

"Success is not final; failure is not fatal:
it is the courage to continue that counts."
Winston S. Churchill

COURAGE

Definition: the ability to do something that is frightening or the strength to persevere in the face of grief, pain, or danger

Before going into battle, Joshua tells his men to have courage. He could have told them anything, but he said, "Be strong and courageous." Life, and specifically "the good life," is not easy and requires courage in public and in private.

This Book of the Law shall not depart from your mouth, but you shall meditate on it day and night, so that you may be careful to do according to all that is written in it. For then you will make your way prosperous, and then you will have good success. Have I not commanded you? Be strong and courageous. Do not be frightened, and do not be dismayed, for the Lord your God is with you wherever you go."
Joshua 1:8-9

Guiding Questions

What person in the Bible, history, literature, or film demonstrated courage?

43

When, why, and how should we (or should we NOT) be courageous?

Vices
Courage can be a virtue in its best and most pure form, but it can quickly become a vice in its extreme form (impulsiveness) or when it is lacking (cowardice). Continue contemplating courage by looking at these two misrepresentations of this virtue.

(+) Impulsiveness
Definition: reaction or action taken without thinking through the consequences or implications for oneself or other

Be not rash with your mouth, nor let your heart be hasty to utter a word before God, for God is in heaven and you are on earth. Therefore, let your words be few.
Ecclesiastes 5:2

(-) Cowardice
Definition: a trait wherein excessive fear prevents an individual from taking a risk or facing danger

The one who conquers will have this heritage, and I will be his God and he will be my son. But as for the cowardly, the faithless, the detestable, as for murderers, the sexually immoral, sorcerers, idolaters, and all liars, their portion will be in the lake that burns with fire and sulfur, which is the second death.
Revelations 21:7-8

Guiding Questions

When have you experienced a person being cowardly or impulsive?

What situations cause you to be cowardly or impulsive?

When have you experienced courage from someone in your life?

How can you cultivate the virtue of courage in your life?

Circle a number to rate yourself in this virtue:

(-) cowardice	Courage	impulsiveness (+)
1 2 3	4 5 4	3 2 1

What kind of person do you want to be?

I am impulsive when...

I am a coward when...

I show courage when...

I want to be...

Cultivating Virtue

Contemplation #8

(-) in deficiency	**VIRTUE**	(+) in excess
indifference	**Curiosity**	meddling

"I have no special talents.
I am only passionately curious."
Albert Einstein

CURIOSITY

Definition: the inquisitive interest in the affairs of others or the operational details and functionality involved in the affairs of the universe

It's good to be curious, but we also need to be ready to follow through on the truth we discover at the end of the path of curiosity. The "Rich Young Ruler" is a great example of showing genuine curiosity, but he lacked the courage to act upon the truth he discovered.

And as he was setting out on his journey, a man ran up and knelt before him and asked him, "Good Teacher, what must I do to inherit eternal life?" And Jesus said to him, "Why do you call me good? No one is good except God alone. You know the commandments: 'Do not murder, Do not commit adultery, Do not steal, Do not bear false witness, Do not defraud, Honor your father and mother.'" And he said to him, "Teacher, all these I have kept from my youth." And Jesus, looking at him, loved him, and said to him, "You lack one thing: go, sell all that you have and give to the poor, and you will have treasure in heaven; and come,

follow me." Disheartened by the saying, he went away
sorrowful, for he had great possessions.
Mark 10:17-22

Guiding Questions

What person in the Bible, history, literature, or film needed
curiosity?

When, why, and how should we (or should we NOT) be
curious to new ideas, circumstances, or surroundings?

Vices
Curiosity can be a virtue in its best and most pure form, but it
can quickly become a vice in its extreme form (meddling) or
when it is lacking (indifference). Continue contemplating
curiosity by looking at these two misrepresentations of this
virtue.

(+) Meddling
Definition: to interfere in or busy oneself unduly with
something that is not one's concern

Whoever meddles in a quarrel not his own is like one who
takes a passing dog by the ears.
Proverbs 26:17

(-) Indifference
Definition: lack of interest, concern, or sympathy

And let us not grow weary of doing good, for in due season
we will reap, if we do not give up.
Galatians 6:9

Guiding Questions

When have you experienced a person being meddling or indifferent?

What situations cause you to be meddling or indifferent?

When have you experienced curiosity from someone in your life?

How can you cultivate the virtue of curiosity in your life?

Circle a number to rate yourself in this virtue:

(-) indifference			Curiosity			meddling (+)		
1	2	3	4	5	4	3	2	1

What kind of person do you want to be?

I am meddling when...

I am indifferent when...

I am curious when...

I want to be...

Cultivating Virtue

Contemplation #9

(-) in deficiency	**VIRTUE**	(+) in excess
fickleness	**Dedication**	mania

"Talent is cheap; dedication is expensive.
It will cost you your life."
Irving Stone

DEDICATION

Definition: a strong desire to do or to achieve something, typically requiring determination and hard work

Life is hard. We have all experienced unexpected setbacks that have altered our plans or inhibited us from achieving a goal. Having dedication when things are not easy is a character trait that makes our life and the lives of those around us better. Being dedicated to loving your spouse, children, parents, or co-workers is equally important to the dedication required to start a new business, maintain a home, or show up to work every day for forty years. In I Corinthians 9, Paul uses the "glamorous" example of athletics to remind us that life is hard, but our dedication will be rewarded.

Do you not know that in a race all the runners run, but only one receives the prize? So run that you may obtain it. Every athlete exercises self-control in all things. They do it to receive a perishable wreath, but we an imperishable. So I do not run aimlessly; I do not box as one beating the air. But I discipline my body and keep it under control, lest after preaching to others I myself should be disqualified.
I Corinthians 9:24-25

51

Guiding Questions

What person in the Bible, history, literature, or film was dedicated?

When, why, and how should we (or should we NOT) be dedicated when facing new ideas, circumstances, or surroundings?

Vices

Dedication can be a virtue in its best and most pure form, but it can quickly become a vice in its extreme form (mania) or when it is lacking (fickleness). Continue contemplating dedication by looking at these two misrepresentations of this virtue.

(+) Mania

Definition: excessive or unreasonable enthusiasm

The heart is deceitful above all things, and desperately sick; who can understand it? "I the Lord search the heart and test the mind, to give every man according to his ways, according to the fruit of his deeds."
Jeremiah 17:9-10

(-) Fickleness

Definition: erratic change caused by a lack of stability, consistency, and steadfastness

And Elijah came near to all the people and said, "How long will you go limping between two different opinions? If the Lord is God, follow him; but if Baal, then follow him." And the people did not answer him a word.
I Kings 18:21

Guiding Questions

When have you experienced a person being manic or fickle?

What situations cause you to be manic or fickle?

When have you experienced dedication from someone in your life?

How can you cultivate the virtue of dedication in your life?

Circle a number to rate yourself in this virtue:

(-) fickleness			Dedication			mania (+)		
1	2	3	4	5	4	3	2	1

What kind of person do you want to be?

I am manic when...

I am fickle when...

I am dedicated when...

I want to be...

53

Cultivating Virtue

Contemplation #10

(-) in deficiency	**VIRTUE**	(+) in excess
unreliability	**Dependability**	stubbornness

"Cultivate dependability
and you will always have responsibilities."
Roy L. Smith

DEPENDABILITY

Definition: capable of being relied on for consistency in character or trusted in accomplishment of a task

Our family has been able to move a few times and live in several areas of the United States. It is a fun adventure to move, but the day you load the moving truck is hard and sometimes stressful. Fortunately, God has always given us a few dependable friends that are willing to take a day or two out of their lives to help us with this exhausting and thankless task. These friends and I are bonded together by that dependability shown during our time of need. Paul's words to the Philippians encouraged a similar lifestyle of consistent dependability among believers.

Only let your manner of life be worthy of the gospel of Christ, so that whether I come and see you or am absent, I may hear of you that you are standing firm in one spirit, with one mind striving side by side for the faith of the gospel, and not frightened in anything by your opponents. This is a clear sign to them of their destruction, but of your salvation, and that from God. For it has been granted to you that for the sake of Christ you should not only believe in him but

also suffer for his sake, engaged in the same conflict that you saw I had and now hear that I still have.
Philippians 1:27-30

Guiding Questions

What person in the Bible, history, literature, or film was dependable?

When, why, and how should we (or should we NOT) be dependable in our actions, reactions, and thoughts?

Vices
Dependability can be a virtue in its best and most pure form, but it can quickly become a vice in its extreme form (stubbornness) or when it is lacking (unreliability). Continue contemplating dependability by looking at these two misrepresentations of this virtue.

(+) Stubbornness
Definition: having or showing dogged determination not to change one's attitude or position on something, especially in spite of good arguments or reasons to do so

Circumcise therefore the foreskin of your heart and be no longer stubborn.
Deuteronomy 10:16

(-) Unreliability
Definition: unstable and not to be trusted or depended on

Whoever can be trusted with very little can also be trusted with much, and whoever is dishonest with very little will also be dishonest with much.
Luke 16:10

Guiding Questions

When have you experienced a person being stubborn or unreliable?

What situations cause you to be stubborn or unreliable?

When have you experienced dependability from someone in your life?

How can you cultivate the virtue of dependability in your life?

Circle a number to rate yourself in this virtue:

(-) unreliability	Dependability	stubbornness (+)
1 2 3	4 5 4	3 2 1

What kind of person do you want to be?

I am stubborn when...

I am unreliable when...

I am dependable when...

I want to be...

Cultivating Virtue

Contemplation #11

(-) in deficiency	**VIRTUE**	(+) in excess
debasement	**Dignity**	gloating

"Human rights rest on human dignity.
The dignity of man is an ideal worth
fighting for and worth dying for."
Robert Maynard

DIGNITY

Definition: formal reservation or seriousness of manner, appearance, or language reflecting worth or quality of being

Humans are created in the image of God. Wow! That is a deep theological truth that is often forgotten or overlooked in the business of our daily life. Without this idea, dignity cannot be achieved. John 13 is often referred to when we talk about service and servant leadership; however, there is also great dignity in the actions and words of Jesus even in the "lowly" act of washing the feet of His followers. This passage also shows the dignity Jesus bestowed on His followers.

When he had washed their feet and put on his outer garments and resumed his place, he said to them, "Do you understand what I have done to you? You call me Teacher and Lord, and you are right, for so I am. If I then, your Lord and Teacher, have washed your feet, you also ought to wash one another's feet. For I have given you an example, that you also should do just as I have done to you. Truly, truly, I say to you, a servant is not greater than his master, nor is a

messenger greater than the one who sent him. If you know
these things, blessed are you if you do them."
John 13:12-17

Guiding Questions

What person in the Bible, history, literature, or film needed
dignity?

When, why, and how should we (or should we NOT) show
dignity to new ideas, circumstances, or surroundings?

Vices
Dignity can be a virtue in its best and most pure form, but it
can quickly become a vice in its extreme form (gloating) or
when it is lacking (debasement). Continue contemplating
dignity by looking at these two misrepresentations of this
virtue.

(+) Gloating
Definition: dwelling on one's own success or another's
misfortune with smugness or malignant pleasure

Do not gloat when your enemy falls; when they stumble, do
not let your heart rejoice.
Proverbs 24:17

(-) Debasement
Definition: the degradation or reduction in quality usually in
relation to moral character or humanity

And since they did not see fit to acknowledge God, God gave
them up to a debased mind to do what ought not to be done.
Romans 1:28

Guiding Questions

When have you experienced a gloating or debased person?

What situations cause you to gloat or be debased?

When have you experienced dignity from someone in your life?

How can you cultivate the virtue of dignity in your life?

Circle a number to rate yourself in this virtue:

(-) debasement	Dignity	gloating (+)
1 2 3	4 5 4	3 2 1

What kind of person do you want to be?

I am gloating when...

I am debased when...

I show dignity when...

I want to be...

Cultivating Virtue

Contemplation #12

(-) in deficiency	**VIRTUE**	(+) in excess
laziness	**Diligence**	workaholism

"He who labors diligently need never despair;
for all things are accomplished by diligence and labor."
Menander

DILIGENCE

Definition: careful and persistent work or effort

I was involved in sports for much of my life, and the idea of diligence was important to the individuals and teams that I coached. Every year, I would see examples of lazy athletes not achieving their potential and diligent athletes' "overachieving" expectations and receiving national recognition. Diligence in our daily lives is the simple idea of waking up every morning and accomplishing our daily tasks at home, work, and church. This consistent daily effort is the overlooked and underrecognized virtue of diligence.

The soul of the sluggard craves and gets nothing, while the soul of the diligent is richly supplied.
Proverbs 13:4

Guiding Questions

What person in the Bible, history, literature, or film needed diligence?

When, why, and how should we (or should we NOT) be diligent in our actions, plans, or surroundings?

Vices

Diligence can be a virtue in its best and most pure form, but it can quickly become a vice in its extreme form (workaholism) or when it is lacking (laziness). Continue contemplating diligence by looking at these two misrepresentations of this virtue.

(+) Workaholism

Definition: a compulsion to work excessively hard and long hours at the expense of personal rest and relationships with other

For everything there is a season, and a time for every matter under heaven: a time to be born, and a time to die; a time to plant, and a time to pluck up what is planted; a time to kill, and a time to heal; a time to break down, and a time to build up; a time to weep, and a time to laugh; a time to mourn, and a time to dance; a time to cast away stones, and a time to gather stones together; a time to embrace, and a time to refrain from embracing; a time to seek, and a time to lose; a time to keep, and a time to cast away; a time to tear, and a time to sew; a time to keep silence, and a time to speak; a time to love, and a time to hate; a time for war, and a time for peace.
Ecclesiastes 3:1-8

(-) Laziness

Definition: the quality of being unwilling to work or use energy; idleness

Go to the ant, O sluggard; consider her ways, and be wise.
Without having any chief, officer, or ruler, she prepares her
bread in summer and gathers her food in harvest.
Proverbs 6:6-8

Guiding Questions

When have you experienced a person being a workaholic or lazy?

What situations cause you to be a workaholic or lazy?

When have you experienced diligence from someone in your life?

How can you cultivate the virtue of diligence in your life?

Circle a number to rate yourself in this virtue:

(-) laziness			Diligence		workaholism (+)		
1	2	3	4	5	4	3	2	1

What kind of person do you want to be?

I am a workaholic when...

I am lazy when...

I am diligent when...

I want to be...

Cultivating Virtue

Contemplation #13

(-) in deficiency	**VIRTUE**	(+) in excess
hardheartedness	**Empathy**	enablement

"Empathy is seeing with the eyes of another,
listening with the ears of another,
and feeling with the heart of another."
Anonymous

EMPATHY

Definition: the ability to place yourself in position of another person; or the ability to understand and feel what another person is presently experiencing and the past experiences that inform their feelings

Modern American culture struggles greatly with the concept of empathy. Thinking of others is difficult but allowing ourselves to care about others long enough to contemplate their past and present experiences so that we can understand how they feel and why they might act in a certain way is almost heretical to the "religion of me" that so many people have joined. Because He is God, Jesus was able to take empathy to the ultimate level of actually becoming human and fully relating to our cares and concerns.

And Jesus went throughout all the cities and villages, teaching in their synagogues and proclaiming the gospel of the kingdom and healing every disease and every affliction. When he saw the crowds, he had compassion for them, because they were harassed and helpless, like sheep without a shepherd. Then he said to his disciples, "The harvest is

67

plentiful, but the laborers are few; therefore pray earnestly to the Lord of the harvest to send out laborers into his harvest." And he called to him his twelve disciples and gave them authority over unclean spirits, to cast them out, and to heal every disease and every affliction.
Matthew 9:35-10:1

Guiding Questions

What person in the Bible, history, literature, or film needed empathy?

When, why, and how should we (or should we NOT) be empathetic to new ideas, circumstances, or surroundings?

Vices
Empathy can be a virtue in its best and most pure form, but it can quickly become a vice in its extreme form (enablement) or when it is lacking (hardheartedness). Continue contemplating by looking at these two misrepresentations of this virtue.

(+) Enablement
Definition: encouraging or enabling negative or self-destructive behavior in another

Let the thief no longer steal, but rather let him labor, doing honest work with his own hands, so that he may have something to share with anyone in need.
Ephesians 4:28

(-) Hardheartedness
Definition: incapable of being moved to pity or tenderness; unfeeling

*Do not withhold good from those to whom it is due, when it
is in your power to do it.
Proverbs 3:27*

Guiding Questions

When have you experienced a person enabling or being
hardhearted?

What situations cause you to be enabling or hardhearted?

When have you experienced empathy from someone in your
life?

How can you cultivate the virtue of empathy in your life?

Circle a number to rate yourself in this virtue:

(-) hardheartedness	**Empathy**	enablement (+)
1 2 3 4	5	4 3 2 1

What kind of person do you want to be?

I am an enabler when...

I am hardhearted when...

I am empathetic when...

I want to be...

Cultivating Virtue

Contemplation #14

(-) in deficiency	**VIRTUE**	(+) in excess
apathy	**Endurance**	obstinacy

*"Come what may, all bad fortune is
to be conquered by endurance."*
Virgil

ENDURANCE

Definition: the ability to withstand hardship or adversity that is unusually prolonged and stressful

I once had a job that required me to be the lynch pin between several distinct organizations. In the first year, there seemed to be no possible way to make anyone happy. The organizations had been thrown together with the idea that they could all work together for a common good, but there were several very strong differing beliefs from multiple factions. Every day, I needed to walk the line between obstinance and apathy to live and work with endurance to bring unity in the midst of diversity for the good of the whole organization. It was the most difficult challenge of my life. However, my "difficult" experience was nothing compared to what Jesus did to save us from our sin.

Therefore, since we are surrounded by so great a cloud of witnesses, let us also lay aside every weight, and sin which clings so closely, and let us run with endurance the race that is set before us, looking to Jesus, the founder and perfecter of our faith, who for the joy that was set before him endured the cross, despising the shame, and is seated at the right

71

hand of the throne of God. Consider him who endured from sinners such hostility against himself, so that you may not grow weary or fainthearted. In your struggle against sin you have not yet resisted to the point of shedding your blood.
Hebrews 12:1-4

Guiding Questions

What person in the Bible, history, literature, or film needed endurance?

When, why, and how should we (or should we NOT) endure with plans, circumstances, or surroundings?

Vices
Endurance can be a virtue in its best and most pure form, but it can quickly become a vice in its extreme form (obstinacy) or when it is lacking (apathy). Continue contemplating endurance by looking at these two misrepresentations of this virtue.

(+) Obstinacy
Definition: stubborn refusal to change one's opinion or chosen course of action, despite attempts to persuade one to do so

Blessed is the one who fears the Lord always, but whoever hardens his heart will fall into calamity.
Proverbs 28:14

(-) Apathy
Definition: showing or feeling no interest, enthusiasm, or concern

Whoever is slack in his work is a brother to him who destroys.
Proverbs 18:9

Guiding Questions

When have you experienced a person being obstinate or apathetic?

What situations cause you to be obstinate or apathetic?

When have you experienced endurance from someone in your life?

How can you cultivate the virtue of endurance in your life?

Circle a number to rate yourself in this virtue:

(-) apathy			**Endurance**			obstinacy (+)		
1	2	3	4	5	4	3	2	1

What kind of person do you want to be?

I am obstinate when...

I am apathetic when...

I show endurance when...

I want to be...

Cultivating Virtue

Contemplation #15

(-) in deficiency	**VIRTUE**	(+) in excess
skepticism	**Faithfulness**	ruthlessness

"A little thing is a little thing, but
faithfulness in little things is a great thing."
James Hudson Taylor

FAITHFULNESS

Definition: steadfast in affection or allegiance

The first time my wife and I left my son at home to take care of our younger children required a lot of faith from us and faithfulness from him. Most of the dinnertime conversation I had with my wife that evening revolved around how the kids were doing and if our son were able to handle this responsibility. When we returned home, we found our son reading a bedtime story to the girls and our other son sound asleep in bed. I am so thankful that we have continued to build on this virtue by giving him more and more responsibility.

"Now after a long time the master of those servants came and settled accounts with them. And he who had received the five talents came forward, bringing five talents more, saying, 'Master, you delivered to me five talents; here, I have made five talents more.' His master said to him, 'Well done, good and faithful servant. You have been faithful over a little; I will set you over much. Enter into the joy of your master.' And he also who had the two talents came forward, saying, 'Master, you delivered to me two talents; here, I have

made two talents more.' His master said to him, 'Well done, good and faithful servant. You have been faithful over a little; I will set you over much. Enter into the joy of your master.' He also who had received the one talent came forward, saying, 'Master, I knew you to be a hard man, reaping where you did not sow, and gathering where you scattered no seed, so I was afraid, and I went and hid your talent in the ground. Here, you have what is yours.' But his master answered him, 'You wicked and slothful servant! You knew that I reap where I have not sown and gather where I scattered no seed? Then you ought to have invested my money with the bankers, and at my coming I should have received what was my own with interest. So, take the talent from him and give it to him who has the ten talents.'"
Matthew 25:19-28

Guiding Questions

What person in the Bible, history, literature, or film needed faithfulness?

When, why, and how should we (or should we NOT) be faithful to new ideas, circumstances, or surroundings?

Vices
Faithfulness can be a virtue in its best and most pure form, but it can quickly become a vice in its extreme form (ruthlessness) or when it is lacking (skepticism). Continue contemplating faithfulness by looking at these two misrepresentations of this virtue.

(+) Ruthlessness
Definition: having or showing no pity or compassion for others to the point of aggressively mean behavior

Let all bitterness and wrath and anger and clamor and slander be put away from you, along with all malice.
Ephesians 4:31

(-) Skepticism
Definition: not easily convinced; having doubts or reservations

Scoffers set a city aflame, but the wise turn away wrath.
Proverbs 29:8

Guiding Questions

When have you experienced a person being ruthless or skeptical?

What situations cause you to be ruthless or skeptical?

When have you experienced faithfulness from someone in your life?

How can you cultivate the virtue of faithfulness in your life?

Circle a number to rate yourself in this virtue:

(-) skepticism	Faithfulness	ruthlessness (+)
1 2 3	4 5 4	3 2 1

What kind of person do you want to be?

I am ruthless when...

I am skeptical when...

I am faithful when...

I want to be...

Cultivating Virtue

Contemplation #16

(-) in deficiency	**VIRTUE**	(+) in excess
rudeness	**Friendliness**	flattery

"Only friendliness produces friendship.
And we must look far deeper into the soul of man
for the thing that produces friendliness."
G.K. Chesterton

FRIENDLINESS

Definition: favorably disposed; inclined to approve, help, or support

Friendliness is often mislabeled as helpful, respectful, politeness, courtesy, or kindness. However, friendliness – as Chesterton said – produces friendship. Take a moment to imagine just how tough the simplest situations in life would become without one or two good friends. Now, consider how often a friend has been a comfort, inspiration, or help to you during a particularly high or low time in life. If you are convicted to work on your friendliness as you think about this, you might also need to contemplate the virtue of gratitude.

Two are better than one, because they have a good reward for their toil. For if they fall, one will lift up his fellow. But woe to him who is alone when he falls and has not another to lift him up! Again, if two lie together, they keep warm, but how can one keep warm alone? And though a man might prevail against one who is alone, two will withstand him—a threefold cord is not quickly broken.
Ecclesiastes 4:9-12

79

Guiding Questions

What person in the Bible, history, literature, or film needed to be friendly?

When, why, and how should we (or should we NOT) be friendly?

Vices

Friendliness can be a virtue in its best and most pure form, but it can quickly become a vice in its extreme form (flattery) or when it is lacking (rudeness). Continue contemplating friendliness by looking at these two misrepresentations of this virtue.

(+) Flattery

Definition: excessive and insincere praise, given especially to further one's own interests

Lead me, O Lord, in your righteousness because of my enemies; make your way straight before me. There is nothing reliable in what they say; Their inward part is destruction itself Their throat is an open grave; They flatter with their tongue.
Psalm 5:8-9

(-) Rudeness

Definition: offensively impolite or ill-mannered with a startling abruptness

To speak evil of no one, to avoid quarreling, to be gentle, and to show perfect courtesy toward all people.
Titus 3:2

Guiding Questions

When have you experienced a person using flattery or being rude?

What situations cause you to be flattering or rude?

When have you experienced friendliness from someone in your life?

How can you cultivate the virtue of friendliness in your life?

Circle a number to rate yourself in this virtue:

(-) rudeness			Friendliness			flattery (+)		
1	2	3	4	5	4	3	2	1

What kind of person do you want to be?

I am flattering when...

I am rude when...

I am friendly when...

I want to be...

Cultivating Virtue

Contemplation #17

(-) in deficiency	**VIRTUE**	(+) in excess
legalism	**Forgiveness**	leniency

"To err is human; to forgive, divine."
Alexander Pope

FORGIVENESS

Definition: the releasing of an offense and no longer keeping record of the wrong someone has done to you or others

As the administrator of a Christian school, I often have the privilege of working with boys who have had a disagreement on the playground. After talking through the situation and asking them to identify what they did wrong, they have the opportunity to ask each other for forgiveness (we talk a lot about repentance, forgiveness, and restoration at our school). When they forgive each other, I often get excited and exclaim, "Do you know what you just did?" The boys inevitably respond by saying, "What?" And this next part is one of my favorite parts of my job. I get to say, "You just acted exactly like Jesus!" As Christians, we talk a lot about living like Jesus, but forgiveness is a fantastic opportunity to actually do it.

Put on then, as God's chosen ones, holy and beloved, compassionate hearts, kindness, humility, meekness, and patience, bearing with one another and, if one has a complaint against another, forgiving each other; as the Lord has forgiven you, so you also must forgive. And above all these put on love, which binds everything together in perfect harmony. And let the peace of Christ rule in your

hearts, to which indeed you were called in one body. And be thankful.
Colossians 3:12-15

Guiding Questions

What person in the Bible, history, literature, or film needed to be forgiving?

When, why, and how should we (or should we NOT) forgive?

Vices
Forgiveness can be a virtue in its best and most pure form, but it can quickly become a vice in its extreme form (leniency) or when it is lacking (legalism). Continue contemplating forgiveness by looking at these two misrepresentations of this virtue.

(+) Leniency
Definition: not as severe or strong in punishment or judgment as would be expected

I warned those who sinned before and all the others, and I warn them now while absent, as I did when present on my second visit, that if I come again I will not spare them.
II Corinthians 13:3

(-) Legalism
Definition: giving too much attention to rules and details

Yet we know that a person is not justified by works of the law but through faith in Jesus Christ, so we also have believed in Christ Jesus, in order to be justified by faith in Christ and not

by works of the law, because by works of the law no one will be justified.
Galatians 2:16

Guiding Questions

When have you experienced a person being lenient or legalistic?

What situations cause you to be overly lenient or legalistic?

When have you experienced forgiveness from someone in your life?

How can you cultivate the virtue of forgiveness in your life?

Circle a number to rate yourself in this virtue:

(-) legalism			**Forgiveness**			leniency (+)		
1	2	3	4	5	4	3	2	1

What kind of person do you want to be?

I am lenient when...

I am legalistic when...

I am forgiving when...

I want to be...

85

Cultivating Virtue

Contemplation #18

(-) in deficiency	**VIRTUE**	(+) in excess
hastiness	**Foresight**	indecisiveness

"The time to repair the roof is when the sun is shining."
John F. Kennedy

FORESIGHT

Definition: the ability to correctly judge what is going to happen

In this high-paced world of microwaves, twitter, text messages, and high-stakes deadlines, it is often hard to find sufficient time to think about the results of our actions before we take them. Foresight is an important virtue to cultivate, but it often goes unnoticed because the bad results that are avoided are never seen, and therefore the good results that are achieved and never fully appreciated.

For the LORD gives wisdom; from his mouth come knowledge and understanding; he stores up sound wisdom for the upright; he is a shield to those who walk in integrity, guarding the paths of justice and watching over the way of his saints. Then you will understand righteousness and justice and equity, every good path; for wisdom will come into your heart, and knowledge will be pleasant to your soul; discretion will watch over you, understanding will guard you, delivering you from the way of evil, from men of perverted speech, who forsake the paths of uprightness to walk in the ways of darkness.
Proverbs 2:6-13

Guiding Questions

What person in the Bible, history, literature, or film needed to use foresight?

When, why, and how should we (or should we NOT) be looking ahead with foresight?

Vices
Foresight can be a virtue in its best and most pure form, but it can quickly become a vice in its extreme form (indecisiveness) or when it is lacking (hastiness). Continue contemplating foresight by looking at these two misrepresentations of this virtue.

(+) Indecisiveness
Definition: the inability to make a decision or take action when presented with more than one option

And Elijah came near to all the people and said, "How long will you go limping between two different opinions? If the Lord is God, follow him; but if Baal, then follow him." And the people did not answer him a word.
I Kings 18:21-22

(-) Hastiness
Definition: actions done in a hurry without appropriate care or thought to possible ramifications

The plans of the diligent lead surely to abundance, but everyone who is hasty comes only to poverty.
Proverbs 21:5

Guiding Questions

When have you experienced a person being indecisive or hasty?

What situations cause you to be indecisive or hasty?

When have you experienced foresight from someone in your life?

How can you cultivate the virtue of foresight in your life?

Circle a number to rate yourself in this virtue:

(-) hastiness	Foresight	indecisiveness (+)
1 2 3	4 5 4	3 2 1

What kind of person do you want to be?

I am indecisive when...

I am hasty when...

I show foresight when...

I want to be...

Cultivating Virtue

Contemplation #19

(-) in deficiency	**VIRTUE**	(+) in excess
timidity	**Fortitude**	obstinacy

"Fortitude is the guard and support of the other virtues."
John Locke

FORTITUDE

Definition: bravery when dealing with pain or difficulty over a long period of time

It is amazing that Jesus came to earth for our salvation, but the way He saved us is even more amazing! It is so fantastic, that to say Isaiah wrote about the "fortitude of Christ" seems reductionistic. However, we learn so much by meditating on God's word with a specific area of growth in mind. Read the following passage and meditate on your own fortitude as compared to that of Christ.

He was oppressed, and he was afflicted, yet he opened not his mouth; like a lamb that is led to the slaughter, and like a sheep that before its shearers is silent, so he opened not his mouth. By oppression and judgment he was taken away; and as for his generation, who considered that he was cut off out of the land of the living, stricken for the transgression of my people? And they made his grave with the wicked and with a rich man in his death, although he had done no violence, and there was no deceit in his mouth.
Isaiah 53:7-9

Guiding Questions

What person in the Bible, history, literature, or film showed fortitude?

When, why, and how should we (or should we NOT) show fortitude?

Vices

Fortitude can be a virtue in its best and most pure form, but it can quickly become a vice in its extreme form (obstinacy) or when it is lacking (timidity). Continue contemplating fortitude by looking at these two misrepresentations of this virtue.

(+) Obstinacy

Definition: unwillingness to change an opinion or action despite persuasive arguments or circumstances

Each man cast down his staff, and they became serpents. But Aaron's staff swallowed up their staffs. Still Pharaoh's heart was hardened, and he would not listen to them, as the Lord had said.
Exodus 7:12-13

(-) Timidity

Definition: the quality of being shy or nervous

For the Spirit God gave us does not make us timid, but gives us power, love and self-discipline.
II Timothy 1:7

Guiding Questions

When have you experienced a person being obstinate or timid?

What situations cause you to be obstinate or timid?

When have you experienced fortitude from someone in your life?

How can you cultivate the virtue of fortitude in your life?

Circle a number to rate yourself in this virtue:

(-) timidity			Fortitude			obstinacy (+)		
1	2	3	4	5	4	3	2	1

What kind of person do you want to be?

I am obstinate when...

I am timid when...

I show fortitude when...

I want to be...

Cultivating Virtue

Contemplation #20

(-) in deficiency	**VIRTUE**	(+) in excess
stinginess	**Generosity**	extravagance

"You have not lived today until you have done
something for someone who can never repay you."
John Bunyan

GENEROSITY

Definition: a willingness to give help or support, especially more than is usual or expected

Generosity reveals a heart full of love, humility, gratitude, and kindness. Love for someone or something is the first and most fundamental reason that draws us into a life of generosity. Another root of this virtue is humility. We have confidence to give to others when we humbly recognize that God gave us everything we have and everything we will ever possess. This humble recognition should naturally fill us with an overwhelmingly generous spirit toward others. However, this generosity does not always have to be with our money. It should also include generosity with our time, ideas, and encouragement. How does this relate to Luke 21:1-4?

Jesus looked up and saw the rich putting their gifts into the offering box, and he saw a poor widow put in two small copper coins. And he said, "Truly, I tell you, this poor widow has put in more than all of them. For they all contributed out of their abundance, but she out of her poverty put in all she had to live on."
Luke 21:1-4

95

Guiding Questions

What person in the Bible, history, literature, or film needed generosity?

When, why, and how should we (or should we NOT) show generosity?

Vices

Generosity can be a virtue in its best and most pure form, but it can quickly become a vice in its extreme form (extravagance) or when it is lacking (stinginess). Continue contemplating generosity by looking at these two misrepresentations of this virtue.

(+) Extravagance

Definition: a lifestyle that is beyond reasonable expectation

Not many days later, the younger son gathered all he had and took a journey into a far country, and there he squandered his property in reckless living.
Luke 15:13

(-) Stinginess

Definition: an unwillingness to spend money or give of one's time or possessions

A stingy man hastens after wealth and does not know that poverty will come upon him.
Proverbs 28:22

Guiding Questions

When have you experienced a person being extravagant or stingy?

What situations cause you to be extravagant or stingy?

When have you experienced generosity from someone in your life?

How can you cultivate the virtue of generosity in your life?

Circle a number to rate yourself in this virtue:

(-) stinginess			Generosity			extravagance (+)		
1	2	3	4	5	4	3	2	1

What kind of person do you want to be?

I am extravagant when...

I am stingy when...

I am generous when...

I want to be...

Cultivating Virtue

Contemplation #21

(-) in deficiency	**VIRTUE**	(+) in excess
angry	**Gentleness***	detachment

"Where anger is a bursting flame,
gentleness is a gentle rain."
Fr. John Harden

GENTLENESS

Definition: the quality of being calm, kind, or soft toward other people

In the quote above, by Fr. Harden, and the Bible verses below, by St. Paul, gentleness is set up as the antidote when we encounter anger, arguments, and evil. Scripture also teaches that a soft or gentle answer turns away wrath (Proverbs 15:1). These reminders are so refreshing to the modern business practices instructing us to respond with equal force if you want to "get ahead" in this world. We are called to a higher and sometimes confusing way of life, but the Holy Spirit will comfort and guide the children of God and produce gentleness in us.

Have nothing to do with foolish, ignorant controversies; you know that they breed quarrels. And the Lord's servant must not be quarrelsome but kind to everyone, able to teach, patiently enduring evil, correcting his opponents with gentleness. God may perhaps grant them repentance leading to a knowledge of the truth.
II Timothy 2:23-25

Guiding Questions

What person in the Bible, history, literature, or film expressed gentleness?

When, why, and how should we (or should we NOT) express gentleness?

Vices

Gentleness can be a virtue in its best and most pure form, but it can quickly become a vice in its extreme form (detachment) or when it is lacking (angry). Continue contemplating gentleness by looking at these two misrepresentations of this virtue.

(+) Detachment

Definition: not emotionally involved in a situation

But if anyone does not provide for his relatives, and especially for members of his household, he has denied the faith and is worse than an unbeliever.
I Timothy 5:8

(-) Angry

Definition: a strong feeling that makes you want to hurt someone or be unpleasant because of something unfair or unkind that has happened

"In your anger do not sin": Do not let the sun go down while you are still angry, and do not give the devil a foothold.
Ephesians 4:26:31

Guiding Questions

When have you experienced a person being detached or angry?

What situations cause you to be detached or angry?

When have you experienced gentleness from someone in your life?

How can you cultivate the virtue of gentleness in your life?

Circle a number to rate yourself in this virtue:

(-) anger			Gentleness*			detachment (+)		
1	2	3	4	5	4	3	2	1

What kind of person do you want to be?

I am detached when...

I show anger when...

I am gentle when...

I want to be...

Cultivating Virtue

Contemplation #22

(-) in deficiency	VIRTUE	(+) in excess
evilness	Goodness*	perfectionism

"Do all the good you can,
By all the means you can, In all the ways you can,
In all the places you can, At all the times you can,
To all the people you can, As long as ever you can."
John Wesley

GOODNESS

Definition: the personal quality of being morally upright or pure

Truth, goodness, and beauty are the transcendentals that a classical Christian education aspires to understand. What is good? Who is good? Why is something or someone good? In Mark 10:18, Jesus tells a rich young man that "no one is good except God alone," but "goodness" is listed as a fruit of the Spirit in Galatians 5:22. When contemplating the virtue of goodness it seems that it is almost interchangeable with the term "virtue" itself. Peter seems to be talking about goodness, or being morally upright and pure, when he writes about the ways in which our faith should grow and build throughout our lives.

For this very reason, make every effort to supplement your faith with virtue, and virtue with knowledge, and knowledge with self-control, and self-control with steadfastness, and steadfastness with godliness, and

godliness with brotherly affection, and brotherly affection with love.
II Peter 1:5-7

Guiding Questions

What person in the Bible, history, literature, or film expressed goodness?

When, why, and how should we (or should we NOT) express goodness?

Vices
Goodness can be a virtue in its best and most pure form, but it can quickly become a vice in its extreme form (perfectionism) or when it is lacking (evilness). Continue contemplating goodness by looking at these two misrepresentations of this virtue.

(+) Perfectionism
Definition: a person who wants very much to get every detail exactly right and is overly demanding of self and others

Do not let your adorning be external (the braiding of hair and the putting on of gold jewelry, or the clothing you wear) but let your adorning be the hidden person of the heart with the imperishable beauty of a gentle and quiet spirit, which in God's sight is very precious.
I Peter 3:3-4

(-) Evilness
Definition: the condition of being immoral, cruel, or bad

Woe to those who call evil good and good evil, who put darkness for light and light for darkness, who put bitter for sweet and sweet for bitter!
Isaiah 5:20

Guiding Questions

When have you experienced a person being perfectionistic or evil?

What situations cause you to be perfectionistic or evil?

When have you experienced goodness from someone in your life?

How can you cultivate the virtue of goodness in your life?

Circle a number to rate yourself in this virtue:

(-) evilness			Goodness*			perfectionism (+)		
1	2	3	4	5	4	3	2	1

What kind of person do you want to be?

I am a perfectionistic when...

I am evil when...

I show goodness when...

I want to be...

Cultivating Virtue

Contemplation #23

(-) in deficiency	**VIRTUE**	(+) in excess
crudeness	**Grace**	indulgence

*"Nothing but grace makes a man so humble
and, at the same time, so glad."*
C.H. Spurgeon

GRACE

Definition: the charming quality of being polite and pleasant, or a willingness to be fair and forgiving

Being fair and forgiving is a difficult virtue to practice in a society that does not always reward this characteristic. In a world dominated by self-promotion and stepping on others to advance a career, it is difficult to exhibit grace. However, if we want to be more like Jesus, we must show grace to others in the same way that He showed grace to us. Forgiveness, mercy, and grace should be the hallmark of any Christian.

Do not be ashamed of the testimony about our Lord, nor of me his prisoner, but share in suffering for the gospel by the power of God, who saved us and called us to a holy calling, not because of our works but because of his own purpose and grace, which he gave us in Christ Jesus before the ages began, and which now has been manifested through the appearing of our Savior Christ Jesus, who abolished death and brought life and immortality to light through the gospel.
II Timothy 1:8-10

107

Guiding Questions

What person in the Bible, history, literature, or film needed grace?

When, why, and how should we (or should we NOT) be gracious?

Vices

Grace can be a virtue in its best and most pure form, but it can quickly become a vice in its extreme form (indulgence) or when it is lacking (crudeness). Continue contemplating grace by looking at these two misrepresentations of this virtue.

(+) Indulgence

Definition: allowing someone to have or do what they want, especially when it is not good for them

Among them we too all formerly lived in the lusts of our flesh, indulging the desires of the flesh and of the mind, and were by nature children of wrath, even as the rest.
Ephesians 2:3

(-) Crudeness

Definition: rude or offensive in speech or action

Let no unwholesome word proceed from your mouth, but only such a word as is good for edification according to the need of the moment, so that it will give grace to those who hear.
Ephesians 4:29

Guiding Questions

When have you experienced a person being indulgent or crude?

What situations cause you to be indulgent or crude?

When have you experienced grace from someone in your life?

How can you cultivate the virtue of grace in your life?

Circle a number to rate yourself in this virtue:

(-) crudeness	Grace	indulgence (+)
1 2 3	4 5 4	3 2 1

What kind of person do you want to be?

I am indulgent when...

I am crude when...

I show grace when...

I want to be...

Cultivating Virtue

Contemplation #24

(-) in deficiency	VIRTUE	(+) in excess
churlishness	**Gratitude**	groveling

"Gratitude is not only the greatest of virtues,
but the parent of all the others."
Cicero

GRATITUDE

Definition: a strong feeling of appreciation for something or to someone for something done for you

While I do not agree with Cicero that gratitude is the parent of all other virtues, I do believe he was making a good point. Gratitude should continually spill out of us in our actions and flow out of us in our speech. We need to recognize that all we have and everything we are is a gift from God. He created us, provides for us, and cares for us in both visible and invisible ways every day. If you know a person who is constantly grateful, most likely you know a person who understands the greatness of God.

And let the peace of Christ rule in your hearts, to which indeed you were called in one body. And be thankful. Let the word of Christ dwell in you richly, teaching and admonishing one another in all wisdom, singing psalms and hymns and spiritual songs, with thankfulness in your hearts to God. And whatever you do, in word or deed, do everything in the name of the Lord Jesus, giving thanks to God the Father through him.
Colossians 3:15-17

Guiding Questions

What person in the Bible, history, literature, or film expressed gratitude?

When, why, and how should we (or should we NOT) be grateful?

Vices
Gratitude can be a virtue in its best and most pure form, but it can quickly become a vice in its extreme form (groveling) or when it is lacking (churlishness). Continue contemplating gratitude by looking at these two misrepresentations of this virtue.

(+) Groveling
Definition: to behave with too much respect toward a person or to act in fear and without self-worth compared to the person being addressed

I will not show partiality to any man or use flattery toward any person. For I do not know how to flatter, else my Maker would soon take me away.
Job 32:21-22

(-) Churlishness
Definition: rude, unfriendly, or unpleasant behavior

Make no friendship with a man given to anger, nor go with a wrathful man.
Proverbs 22:24

Guiding Questions

When have you experienced a person groveling or being rude?

What situations cause you to grovel or express rudeness?

When have you experienced gratitude from someone in your life?

How can you cultivate the virtue of gratitude in your life?

Circle a number to rate yourself in this virtue:

(-) churlishness	Gratitude	groveling (+)
1 2 3	4 5 4	3 2 1

What kind of person do you want to be?

I am groveling when...

I am churlish when...

I am grateful when...

I want to be...

Cultivating Virtue

Contemplation #25

(-) in deficiency	VIRTUE	(+) in excess
deceitfulness	Honesty	outspokenness

"Honesty is the first chapter in the book of wisdom."
Thomas Jefferson

HONESTY

Definition: the quality of speaking and acting truthfully

Most of us think of what we say when we contemplate honesty. However, honesty can sometimes be much more intertwined with our actions than our speech. Consider Paul's observations in the second chapter of Romans. We often make true statements and then act in ways that directly contradict our words. So, consider honesty in light of your actions not just your words.

You then who teach others, do you not teach yourself? While you preach against stealing, do you steal? You who say that one must not commit adultery, do you commit adultery? You who abhor idols, do you rob temples? You who boast in the law dishonor God by breaking the law. For, as it is written, "The name of God is blasphemed among the Gentiles because of you."
Romans 2:21-24

Guiding Questions

What person in the Bible, history, literature, or film needed honesty?

115

When, why, and how should we (or should we NOT) be honest?

Vices

Honesty can be a virtue in its best and most pure form, but it can quickly become a vice in its extreme form (outspokenness) or when it is lacking (deceitfulness). Continue contemplating honesty by looking at these two misrepresentations of this virtue.

(+) Outspokenness

Definition: expressing strong opinions very directly without worrying if other people are offended

The Lord will fight for you, and you have only to be silent."
Exodus 14:14

(-) Deceitfulness

Definition: speech or behavior that keeps the truth hidden

So put away all malice and all deceit and hypocrisy and envy and all slander.
I Peter 2:1

Guiding Questions

When have you experienced a person being outspoken or deceitful?

What situations cause you to be outspoken or deceitful?

When have you experienced honesty from someone in your life?

How can you cultivate the virtue of honesty in your life?

Circle a number to rate yourself in this virtue:

(-) deceitfulness	Honesty	outspokenness (+)
1 2 3	4 5 4	3 2 1

What kind of person do you want to be?

I am outspoken when...

I am deceitful when...

I am honest when...

I want to be...

Cultivating Virtue

Contemplation #26

(-) in deficiency	**VIRTUE**	(+) in excess
negligence	**Honor**	controlling

*"I would prefer even to
fail with honor than win by cheating."*
Sophocles

HONOR

Definition: a good character or reputation for honesty and fair dealing

In Proverbs 22:1, we read that having a good name is more important than wealth, and being given honor is more valuable then gold or silver. Arthur Miller does a good job of presenting this idea in *The Crucible,* a play based on the witchcraft trials in Salem, Massachusetts, from the late 1600's. At the end of the play, John Proctor must make a choice between telling the truth and being put to death or telling a lie and being allowed to live. He will not sign his name to a false confession and cries out, "Because it is my name! Because I cannot have another in my life!" This is the passion we should have to build and protect our own honor and the honor of others through a lifetime of righteous words and actions.

Honor your father and your mother, as the Lord your God commanded you, that your days may be long, and that it may go well with you in the land that the Lord your God is giving you.
Deuteronomy 5:16

Guiding Questions

What person in the Bible, history, literature, or film needed honor?

When, why, and how should we (or should we NOT) be honorable?

Vices

Honor can be a virtue in its best and most pure form, but it can quickly become a vice in its extreme form (controlling) or when it is lacking (negligence). Continue contemplating honor by looking at these two misrepresentations of this virtue.

(+) Controlling

Definition: to strongly influence the way in which something will happen, or someone will behave with the intent of gaining unmerited personal benefit of glory

I appeal to you, brothers, to watch out for those who cause divisions and create obstacles contrary to the doctrine that you have been taught; avoid them. For such persons do not serve our Lord Christ, but their own appetites, and by smooth talk and flattery they deceive the hearts of the naive.
Romans 16:17-18

(-) Negligence

Definition: not giving enough care or attention to something

Woe to you, scribes and Pharisees, hypocrites! For you tithe mint and dill and cumin, and have neglected the weightier matters of the law: justice and mercy and faithfulness. These you ought to have done, without neglecting the others.
Matthew 23:23

Guiding Questions

When have you experienced a person being controlling or negligent?

What situations cause you to be controlling or negligent?

When have you experienced honor from someone in your life?

How can you cultivate the virtue of honor in your life?

Circle a number to rate yourself in this virtue:

(-) negligence			Honor			controlling (+)		
1	2	3	4	5	4	3	2	1

What kind of person do you want to be?

I am controlling when...

I am negligent when...

I am honorable when...

I want to be...

Cultivating Virtue

Contemplation #27

(-) in deficiency	**VIRTUE**	(+) in excess
pessimism	**Hope**	naivety

"We must accept finite disappointment,
but never lose infinite hope."
Martin Luther King Jr.

HOPE

Definition: to want something to happen or to be true, and usually have a good reason to think that it might

Hope is more than a wish. Hope is the convergence of a lifetime of knowledge and experiences that produce a foundation of confidence on which a person can stand. Consider the following statements, 1) I hope I win the lottery, 2) I hope our football team wins, 3) I hope I get a new bike for Christmas, 4) I hope my daughter marries a good man, 5) I hope the Lord returns soon. Which of these statements can be supported by the most confident hope?

Therefore, since we have been justified by faith, we have peace with God through our Lord Jesus Christ. Through him we have also obtained access by faith into this grace in which we stand, and we rejoice in hope of the glory of God. Not only that, but we rejoice in our sufferings, knowing that suffering produces endurance, and endurance produces character, and character produces hope, and hope does not put us to shame, because God's love has been poured into our hearts through the Holy Spirit who has been given to us.
Romans 5:1-5

Guiding Questions

What person in the Bible, history, literature, or film needed hope?

When, why, and how should we (or should we NOT) be hopeful?

Vices
Hope can be a virtue in its best and most pure form, but it can quickly become a vice in its extreme form (naivety) or when it is lacking (pessimism). Continue contemplating hope by looking at these two misrepresentations of this virtue.

(+) Naivety
Definition: too readily believing someone or something without reason or experience

The simple believes everything, but the prudent gives thought to his steps.
Proverbs 14:15

(-) Pessimism
Definition: thinking that bad things are more likely to happen or to emphasize the bad part of a situation

But the mountain falls and crumbles away, and the rock is removed from its place; the waters wear away the stones; the torrents wash away the soil of the earth; so you destroy the hope of man.
Job 14:18-19

Guiding Questions

When have you experienced a person being naive or pessimistic?

What situations cause you to be naive or pessimistic??

When have you experienced hope from someone in your life?

How can you cultivate the virtue of hope in your life?

Circle a number to rate yourself in this virtue:

(-) pessimism	Hope	naivety (+)
1 2 3	4 5 4	3 2 1

What kind of person do you want to be?

I am naive when...

I am pessimistic when...

I am hopeful when...

I want to be...

Cultivating Virtue

Contemplation #28

(-) in deficiency	**VIRTUE**	(+) in excess
aloofness	**Hospitality**	stifling

"A man of substance dear to his fellows for his dwelling
was by the road-side and he entertained all men."
Homer, from The Iliad, Book VI

HOSPITALITY

Definition: friendly or welcoming to guests, visitors, or strangers

In Acts 16, we read about the hospitality of a jailor toward Paul and Silas. The jailor gave them food and cared for their injuries. Hospitality involved caring for the needs of other people. As we seek to do this well throughout our lives, we need to find the balance between stifling people with too much care and attention that would make them feel overwhelmed and uncomfortable, and being aloof and only providing the most minimal care for them so that they could think they are an inconvenience to us. The "golden mean" between these too characteristics is a love for others that results in genuine care and hospitality.

And he took them the same hour of the night and washed their wounds; and he was baptized at once, he and all his family. Then he brought them up into his house and set food before them. And he rejoiced along with his entire household that he had believed in God.
Acts 16:33-34

Guiding Questions

What person in the Bible, history, literature, or film needed to be hospitable?

When, why, and how should we (or should we NOT) be hospitable?

Vices
Hospitality can be a virtue in its best and most pure form, but it can quickly become a vice in its extreme form (stifling) or when it is lacking (aloofness). Continue contemplating showing hospitality by looking at these two misrepresentations of this virtue.

(+) Stifling
Definition: being overly involved with a person in a way that prevents someone from fully enjoying life or acting as they would like to act

Know this, my beloved brothers: let every person be quick to hear, slow to speak, slow to anger.
James 1:19

(-) Aloofness
Definition: not friendly or willing to take part in things with other people

They abhor me; they keep aloof from me; they do not hesitate to spit at the sight of me.
Job 30:10

Guiding Questions

When have you experienced a person being stifling or aloof?

What situations cause you to be stifling or aloof?

When have you experienced hospitality from someone in your life?

How can you cultivate the virtue of hospitality in your life?

Circle a number to rate yourself in this virtue:

(-) aloofness			Hospitality			stifling (+)		
1	2	3	4	5	4	3	2	1

What kind of person do you want to be?

I am stifling when...

I am aloof when...

I am hospitable when...

I want to be...

Cultivating Virtue

Contemplation #29

(-) in deficiency	VIRTUE	(+) in excess
pride	Humility	degradation

"Humility is not thinking less of yourself,
it's thinking of yourself less."
C. S. Lewis

HUMILITY

Definition: the feeling or attitude that you have no special importance or entitlement to anything more than you currently have

Seeking to exalt ourselves will only lead to our demise. We do not have the power or understanding of the interconnectivity of all things that is required to raise ourselves up to a place of prominence. However, God makes a great promise to us that genuine humility could, in due time, result in Him raising us up. It has often been said that a lot can be accomplished when no one cares who gets the credit, but a better twist on that thought is that a lot can be accomplished when everyone cares that only God receives the credit and glory.

Likewise, you who are younger, be subject to the elders. Clothe yourselves, all of you, with humility toward one another, for "God opposes the proud but gives grace to the humble." Humble yourselves, therefore, under the mighty hand of God so that at the proper time he may exalt you, casting all your anxieties on him, because he cares for you.
I Peter 5:5-7

131

Guiding Questions

What person in the Bible, history, literature, or film needed humility?

When, why, and how should we (or should we NOT) show humility?

Vices

Humility can be a virtue in its best and most pure form, but it can quickly become a vice in its extreme form (degradation) or when it is lacking (pride). Continue contemplating humility by looking at these two misrepresentations of this virtue.

(+) Degradation

Definition: seeming to be worthless or without the need of respect from other

For you formed my inward parts; you knitted me together in my mother's womb. I praise you, for I am fearfully and wonderfully made. Wonderful are your works; my soul knows it very well.
Psalm 139:13-14

(-) Pride

Definition: the belief of being better or more important than other people

The eyes of the arrogant will be humbled and human pride brought low; the Lord alone will be exalted in that day. The Lord Almighty has a day in store for all the proud and lofty, for all that is exalted (and they will be humbled).
Isaiah 2:11-12

Guiding Questions

When have you experienced a person being degrading or prideful?

What situations cause you to be degrading or prideful?

When have you experienced humility from someone in your life?

How can you cultivate the virtue of humility in your life?

Circle a number to rate yourself in this virtue:

(-) pride			Humility		degradation (+)		
1	2	3	4	5	4	3	2	1

What kind of person do you want to be?

I am degrading when...

I am prideful when...

I am humble when...

I want to be...

Cultivating Virtue

Contemplation #30

(-) in deficiency	**VIRTUE**	(+) in excess
laziness	**Industriousness**	workaholism

"Some temptations come to the industrious,
but all temptations attack the idle."
Charles Spurgeon

INDUSTRIOUSNESS

Definition: characterized by earnest, diligent, and steady effort and hard work

Industriousness can often be a great equalizer amongst peers with various levels of talent. I found this to be true when I coached college wrestling. There were numerous examples of more talented wrestlers being surpassed and losing their varsity spot to individuals with lesser skills but who had diligently logged extra hours of effort to improve their skills every day. Each of us should seek to cultivate industriousness in our own lives so that we can effectively accomplish the good works that God has prepared for us to do.

My son, if you have put up security for your neighbor, have given your pledge for a stranger, if you are snared in the words of your mouth, caught in the words of your mouth, then do this, my son, and save yourself, for you have come into the hand of your neighbor: go, hasten, and plead urgently with your neighbor. Give your eyes no sleep and your eyelids no slumber; save yourself like a gazelle from the hand of the hunter, like a bird from the hand of the fowler.
Proverbs 6:1-5

Guiding Questions

What person in the Bible, history, literature, or film needed to be industrious?

When, why, and how should we (or should we NOT) be industrious?

Vices
Industriousness can be a virtue in its best and most pure form, but it can quickly become a vice in its extreme form (workaholism) or when it is lacking (laziness). Continue contemplating industriousness by looking at these two misrepresentations of this virtue.

(+) Workaholism
Definition: a feeling of compulsion to work excessively

Unless the Lord builds the house, those who build it labor in vain. Unless the Lord watches over the city, the watchman stays awake in vain. It is in vain that you rise up early and go late to rest, eating the bread of anxious toil; for he gives to his beloved sleep.
Psalm 127:1-2

(-) Laziness
Definition: not eager or willing to work or exert oneself

Lazy hands make for poverty, but diligent hands bring wealth.
Proverbs 10:4

Guiding Questions

When have you experienced a person being a workaholic or lazy?

What situations cause you to be a workaholic or lazy?

When have you experienced industriousness from someone in your life?

How can you cultivate the virtue of industriousness in your life?

Circle a number to rate yourself in this virtue:

(-) laziness			**Industriousness**		workaholism (+)		
1	2	3	4	5	4	3	2	1

What kind of person do you want to be?

I am a workaholic when...

I am lazy when...

I am industrious when...

I want to be...

Cultivating Virtue

Contemplation #31

(-) in deficiency	**VIRTUE**	(+) in excess
corruption	**Integrity**	legalism

"Subtlety may deceive you; integrity never will."
Oliver Cromwell

INTEGRITY

Definition: a firm adherence to a code of established moral or artistic values that are followed in public and in private

Semper fidelis (shortened to *semper fi*) is the moto of the United States Marine Corps. This Latin phrase means "always faithful" and is a significant part of the strict code of a Marine. Living by an established moral code helps a person to live within the boundaries of integrity. However, to have true integrity, you must also change from within so that your belief and desire matches the external actions leading to integrity. This change requires contemplation of the good life, cultivation of virtue, and daily effort to improve every area of your life.

Keep your heart with all vigilance, for from it flow the springs of life. Put away from you crooked speech, and put devious talk far from you. Let your eyes look directly forward, and your gaze be straight before you. Ponder the path of your feet; then all your ways will be sure. Do not swerve to the right or to the left; turn your foot away from evil.
Proverbs 4:23-27

Guiding Questions

What person in the Bible, history, literature, or film needed integrity?

When, why, and how should we (or should we NOT) have integrity?

Vices

Integrity can be a virtue in its best and most pure form, but it can quickly become a vice in its extreme form (legalism) or when it is lacking (corruption). Continue contemplating integrity by looking at these two misrepresentations of this virtue.

(+) Legalism

Definition: an excessively strict and literal conformity to the law a religious or moral code

For whoever keeps the whole law but fails in one point has become accountable for all of it.
James 2:10

(-) Corruption

Definition: dishonest or illegal behavior especially by powerful people

For the one who sows to his own flesh will from the flesh reap corruption, but the one who sows to the Spirit will from the Spirit reap eternal life.
Galatians 6:8

Guiding Questions

When have you experienced a person being legalistic or corrupt?

What situations cause you to be legalistic or corrupt?

When have you experienced integrity from someone in your life?

How can you cultivate the virtue of integrity in your life?

Circle a number to rate yourself in this virtue:

(-) corruption			Integrity			legalism (+)		
1	2	3	4	5	4	3	2	1

What kind of person do you want to be?

I am legalistic when...

I am corrupt when...

I show integrity when...

I want to be...

Cultivating Virtue

Contemplation #32

(-) in deficiency	VIRTUE	(+) in excess
apathy	Joy*	flamboyance

*"Joy does not simply happen to us.
We have to choose joy and keep choosing it every day."
Henri Nouwen*

JOY

Definition: the emotion evoked by well-being, success, or good fortune or by the prospect of possessing what one desires

God gave us emotions and built them into us for our good and His glory. However, if we are overly emotional, it can be detrimental to our relationships or our own personal development. Being flamboyant, or showy, can build a false wall or push others away from developing a genuine relationship with us. In the same way, we build a false wall and pull ourselves away from genuine relationships when we allow ourselves to become apathetic. True joy is the balance we need in our emotions, and it also produces strength and purpose throughout life.

He who sires a fool gets himself sorrow, and the father of a fool has no joy. A joyful heart is good medicine, but a crushed spirit dries up the bones. The wicked accepts a bribe in secret to pervert the ways of justice.
Proverbs 17:21-23

143

Guiding Questions

What person in the Bible, history, literature, or film needed joy?

When, why, and how should we (or should we NOT) be joyful?

Vices
Joy can be a virtue in its best and most pure form, but it can quickly become a vice in its extreme form (flamboyance) or when it is lacking (apathy). Continue contemplating joy by looking at these two misrepresentations of this virtue.

(+) Flamboyance
Definition: being overly expressive or emotional with the intention of drawing attention to yourself

And Jesus, looking at him, loved him, and said to him, "You lack one thing: go, sell all that you have and give to the poor, and you will have treasure in heaven; and come, follow me." Disheartened by the saying, he went away sorrowful, for he had great possessions. And Jesus looked around and said to his disciples, "How difficult it will be for those who have wealth to enter the kingdom of God!" And the disciples were amazed at his words.
Mark 10:21-24

(-) Apathy
Definition: a lack emotional attachment or feelings

Whoever isolates himself seeks his own desire; he breaks out against all sound judgment.
Proverbs 18:1

Guiding Questions

When have you experienced a person being flamboyant or apathetic?

What situations cause you to be flamboyant or apathetic?

When have you experienced joy from someone in your life?

How can you cultivate the virtue of joy in your life?

Circle a number to rate yourself in this virtue:

(-) apathy			Joy*			flamboyance (+)		
1	2	3	4	5	4	3	2	1

What kind of person do you want to be?

I am flamboyant when...

I show apathy when...

I am joyful when...

I want to be...

Cultivating Virtue

Contemplation #33

(-) in deficiency	VIRTUE	(+) in excess
corruption	Justice	detachment

"Justice without mercy is cruelty."
Saint Thomas Aquinas

JUSTICE

Definition: the condition of being morally correct or fair

In Micah 6:8, we learn that God has shown us what is good and what is required of us. We are instructed to do (or act) justly but to love mercy. This is a profound statement that is echoed in our opening quote by Thomas Aquinas reflecting on the constant tension between justice and mercy. Solomon expounds on the idea of justice and corruption supporting evil in the following verses and ends the contemplation by instructing us to confront evil. He promises that a blessing of goodness will be our reward for confronting evil with justice. One of the blessings will be the cultivation of courage.

Partiality in judging is not good. Whoever says to the wicked, "You are in the right," will be cursed by peoples, abhorred by nations, but those who rebuke the wicked will have delight, and a good blessing will come upon them.
Proverbs 24:23-25

Guiding Questions

What person in the Bible, history, literature, or film needed justice?

147

When, why, and how should we (or should we NOT) be just?

Vices
Justice can be a virtue in its best and most pure form, but it can quickly become a vice in its extreme form (detachment) or when it is lacking (corruption). Continue contemplating justice by looking at these two misrepresentations of this virtue.

(+) Detachment
Definition: not emotionally involved in a situation or with people

The LORD is near to the brokenhearted and saves the crushed in spirit.
Psalm 34:18

(-) Corruption
Definition: the change from good to bad in morals, manners, or actions

Yet his sons did not walk in his ways but turned aside after gain. They took bribes and perverted justice. Then all the elders of Israel gathered together and came to Samuel at Ramah 5 and said to him, "Behold, you are old and your sons do not walk in your ways. Now appoint for us a king to judge us like all the nations." But the thing displeased Samuel when they said, "Give us a king to judge us."
I Samuel 8:3-6

Guiding Questions

When have you experienced a person being detached or corrupt?

What situations cause you to be detached or corrupt?

When have you experienced justice from someone in your life?

How can you cultivate the virtue of justice in your life?

Circle a number to rate yourself in this virtue:

(-) corruption				Justice		detachment (+)		
1	2	3	4	5	4	3	2	1

What kind of person do you want to be?

I am detached when...

I am corrupt when...

I show justice when...

I want to be...

Cultivating Virtue

Contemplation #34

(-) in deficiency	**VIRTUE**	(+) in excess
hostility	**Kindness***	foolishness

*"He who sows courtesy reaps friendship,
and he who plants kindness gathers love."*
St. Basil

KINDNESS

Definition: the quality of being generous, helpful, and caring about other people

I was talking to one of my friends recently who owns several restaurants, and he told me that he trains all his staff members to operate by one simple rule. "Just be kind!" This simple rule has served him and his employees well, and he continues to add more restaurants to his portfolio. We would all do well, and most likely become more virtuous in other ways if we followed this one simple rule in our own personal lives. Try living by this simple rule for the next week and see what happens when you decide to "just be kind."

But when the goodness and loving kindness of God our Savior appeared, he saved us, not because of works done by us in righteousness, but according to his own mercy, by the washing of regeneration and renewal of the Holy Spirit, whom he poured out on us richly through Jesus Christ our Savior, so that being justified by his grace we might become heirs according to the hope of eternal life.
Titus 3:4-7

Guiding Questions

What person in the Bible, history, literature, or film needed to be kind?

When, why, and how should we (or should we NOT) be kind?

Vices
Kindness can be a virtue in its best and most pure form, but it can quickly become a vice in its extreme form (foolishness) or when it is lacking (hostility). Continue contemplating kindness by looking at these two misrepresentations of this virtue.

(+) Foolishness
Definition: unwise, stupid, or not showing good judgment

My wounds stink and fester because of my foolishness.
Psalm 38:5

(-) Hostility
Definition: being unfriendly to the point of showing a strong dislike toward someone in your actions or words

Your kindness will reward you, but your cruelty will destroy you.
Proverbs 11:17

Guiding Questions

When have you experienced a person being foolish or hostile?

What situations cause you to be foolish or hostile?

When have you experienced kindness from someone in your life?

How can you cultivate the virtue of kindness in your life?

Circle a number to rate yourself in this virtue:

(-) hostility			Kindness*			foolishness (+)		
1	2	3	4	5	4	3	2	1

What kind of person do you want to be?

I am foolish when...

I am hostile when...

I am kind when...

I want to be...

Cultivating Virtue

Contemplation #35

(-) in deficiency	**VIRTUE**	(+) in excess
selfishness	**Love***	permissiveness

"Love is a friendship set to music."
Joseph Campbell

LOVE

Definition: to have a strong affection for someone

When you are rooted and grounded in true, good, and beautiful love, as described in Ephesians 3:16-19, it is easier to cultivate every other virtue. A love that is grounded in God the Father, Son, and Spirit is the foundation from which all other virtues can be cultivated and gain lifelong nourishment. A love like this is described in I Corinthians 13:3-8. Looking at the descriptions of love in these verses, we see that love produces the virtues patience, kindness, contentment, humility, curiosity, friendliness, adaptivity, forgiveness, joy, truthfulness, servanthood, faithfulness, hope, endurance, and dependability.

If I give away all I have, and if I deliver up my body to be burned, but have not love, I gain nothing. Love is patient and kind; love does not envy or boast; it is not arrogant or rude. It does not insist on its own way; it is not irritable or resentful; it does not rejoice at wrongdoing, but rejoices with the truth. Love bears all things, believes all things, hopes all things, endures all things. Love never ends.
I Corinthians 13:3-8

155

Guiding Questions

What person in the Bible, history, literature, or film needed love?

When, why, and how should we (or should we NOT) love?

Vices
Love can be a virtue in its best and most pure form, but it can quickly become a vice in its extreme form (permissiveness) or when it is lacking (selfishness). Continue contemplating love by looking at these two misrepresentations of this virtue.

(+) Permissiveness
Definition: allowing a wide range of choices, especially in an area where there have traditionally been rules that had to be obeyed

For the moment all discipline seems painful rather than pleasant, but later it yields the peaceful fruit of righteousness to those who have been trained by it.
Hebrews 12:11

(-) Selfishness
Definition: a concern for one's own welfare or advantage at the expense of or in disregard of others

For where jealousy and selfish ambition exist, there will be disorder and every vile practice.
James 3:16

Guiding Questions

When have you experienced a person being permissive or selfish?

What situations cause you to be permissive or selfish?

When have you experienced love from someone in your life?

How can you cultivate the virtue of love in your life?

Circle a number to rate yourself in this virtue:

(-) selfishness				Love*		permissiveness (+)		
1	2	3	4	5	4	3	2	1

What kind of person do you want to be?

I am permissive when...

I am selfish when...

I am loving when...

I want to be...

157

Cultivating Virtue

Contemplation #36

(-) in deficiency	**VIRTUE**	(+) in excess
treachery	**Loyalty**	thoughtlessness

*"Loyalty means nothing unless it has at its
heart the absolute principle of self-sacrifice."*
Woodrow T. Wilson

LOYALTY

Definition: faithful to a person to whom faithfulness is due

We all have someone to whom we are loyal, but it can be a struggle to determine how far to extend our loyalty. David determined to be loyal to a dishonest king who tried to kill him. King Saul also convinced others to attempt to harm David as well. David, however, quietly remained loyal to Saul and sought his good.

He said to his men, "The Lord forbid that I should do this thing to my lord, the Lord's anointed, to put out my hand against him, seeing he is the Lord's anointed." So David persuaded his men with these words and did not permit them to attack Saul. And Saul rose up and left the cave and went on his way. Afterward David also arose and went out of the cave, and called after Saul, "My lord the king!" And when Saul looked behind him, David bowed with his face to the earth and paid homage. And David said to Saul, "Why do you listen to the words of men who say, 'Behold, David seeks your harm'? Behold, this day your eyes have seen how the Lord gave you today into my hand in the cave. And some

told me to kill you, but I spared you. I said, 'I will not put out
my hand against my lord, for he is the Lord's anointed.'
I Samuel 24:6-10

Guiding Questions

What person in the Bible, history, literature, or film needed
loyalty?

When, why, and how should we (or should we NOT) be
loyal?

Vices
Loyalty can be a virtue in its best and most pure form, but it
can quickly become a vice in its extreme form
(thoughtlessness) or when it is lacking (treachery). Continue
contemplating loyalty by looking at these two
misrepresentations of this virtue.

(+) Thoughtlessness
Definition: lacking concern for others

Thoughtless words cut like a sword. But the tongue of wise
people brings healing.
Proverbs 12:18

(-) Treachery
Definition: violation of allegiance, faith, or confidence

The integrity of the upright guides them, but the crookedness
of the treacherous destroys them.
Proverbs 11:3

Guiding Questions

When have you experienced a person being thoughtless or treacherous?

What situations cause you to be thoughtless or treacherous?

When have you experienced loyalty from someone in your life?

How can you cultivate the virtue of loyalty in your life?

Circle a number to rate yourself in this virtue:

(-) treachery			Loyalty			thoughtlessness (+)		
1	2	3	4	5	4	3	2	1

What kind of person do you want to be?

I am thoughtless when...

I am treacherous when...

I am loyal when...

I want to be...

Cultivating Virtue

Contemplation #37

(-) in deficiency	**VIRTUE**	(+) in excess
arrogance	**Meekness**	timidity

"A meek man enjoys almost a perpetual Sabbath."
Philip Henry

MEEKNESS

Definition: a mild, moderate, humble, or submissive quality

Our modern culture has associated meekness with weakness, but Jesus teaches that the meek will inherit the earth. Meekness is the golden mean between timidity and arrogance and is most closely related to humility. Meekness can only be achieved by a person who contemplates and understands the greatness of our almighty God in relation to the finiteness of humanity.

Seeing the crowds, he went up on the mountain, and when he sat down, his disciples came to him. And he opened his mouth and taught them, saying: Blessed are the poor in spirit, for theirs is the kingdom of heaven. Blessed are those who mourn, for they shall be comforted. Blessed are the meek, for they shall inherit the earth. Blessed are those who hunger and thirst for righteousness, for they shall be satisfied. Blessed are the merciful, for they shall receive mercy. Blessed are the pure in heart, for they shall see God. Blessed are the peacemakers, for they shall be called sons of God. Blessed are those who are persecuted for righteousness' sake, for theirs is the kingdom of heaven. Blessed are you

when others revile you and persecute you and utter all kinds of evil against you falsely on my account.
Matthew 5:1-11

Guiding Questions

What person in the Bible, history, literature, or film needed meekness?

When, why, and how should we (or should we NOT) be meek?

Vices

Meekness can be a virtue in its best and most pure form, but it can quickly become a vice in its extreme form (timidity) or when it is lacking (arrogance). Continue contemplating meekness by looking at these two misrepresentations of this virtue.

(+) Timidity

Definition: lacking in courage or self-confidence

For God has not given us a spirit of timidity, but of power and love and discipline.
II Timothy 1:7

(-) Arrogance

Definition: an attitude of superiority manifested in an overbearing manner or in presumptuous claims or assumptions

The fear of the Lord is hatred of evil. Pride and arrogance and the way of evil and perverted speech I hate.
Proverbs 8:13

Guiding Questions

When have you experienced a person being timid or arrogant?

What situations cause you to be timid or arrogant?

When have you experienced meekness from someone in your life?

How can you cultivate the virtue of meekness in your life?

Circle a number to rate yourself in this virtue:

(-) arrogance			Meekness			timidity (+)		
1	2	3	4	5	4	3	2	1

What kind of person do you want to be?

I am timid when...

I am arrogant when...

I am meek when...

I want to be...

Cultivating Virtue

Contemplation #38

(-) in deficiency	VIRTUE	(+) in excess
cruelty	Mercy	shamefulness

"Mercy, detached from justice, grows unmerciful."
C.S. Lewis

MERCY

Definition: compassionate treatment of individual offenders of a law or toward those in distress

The following verses in Micah give us such a beautifully poetic picture of mercy. The idea that God delights in love so much that He will not stay angry at us and will show us mercy is awesome! If our holy God can show mercy to us, how much more should we be merciful to others? How can we possibly find a way to perfectly balance justice, mercy, loyalty, courage, and all the other virtues? At this point, you have studied enough virtues to appreciate our great Father in Heaven, Savior Jesus, and Holy Spirit who perfectly demonstrate the balance of all virtues without allowing one virtue to tip the scales of another toward vice. Consider how you can be more merciful today.

Who is a God like you, pardoning iniquity and passing over transgression for the remnant of his inheritance? He does not retain his anger forever, because he delights in steadfast love. He will again have compassion on us; he will tread our iniquities underfoot. You will cast all our sins into the depths of the sea.
Micah 7:18-19

Guiding Questions

What person in the Bible, history, literature, or film needed mercy?

When, why, and how should we (or should we NOT) show mercy?

Vices

Mercy can be a virtue in its best and most pure form, but it can quickly become a vice in its extreme form (shamefulness) or when it is lacking (cruelty). Continue contemplating mercy by looking at these two misrepresentations of this virtue.

(+) Shamefulness

Definition: an uncomfortable feeling of guilt resulting from your own or someone else's bad behavior

O Lord, let me not be put to shame, for I call upon you; let the wicked be put to shame; let them go silently to Sheol.
Psalm 31:17

(-) Cruelty

Definition: inhuman treatment or punishment

A righteous man has regard for the life of his animal, but even the compassion of the wicked is cruel.
Proverbs 12:10

Guiding Questions

When have you experienced a person being shameful or cruel?

What situations cause you to be shameful or cruel?

When have you experienced mercy from someone in your life?

How can you cultivate the virtue of mercy in your life?

Circle a number to rate yourself in this virtue:

(-) cruelty	Mercy	shamefulness (+)
1 2 3	4 5 4	3 2 1

What kind of person do you want to be?

I am shameful when...

I am cruel when...

I show mercy when...

I want to be...

Cultivating Virtue

Contemplation #39

(-) in deficiency	VIRTUE	(+) in excess
shamelessness	**Modesty**	shyness

"I have often wished I had time to cultivate modesty.
But I am too busy thinking about myself."
Edith Sitwell

MODESTY

Definition: the quality of not being too proud or confident about yourself or your abilities

Our modern culture has begun to use the word *modesty* almost exclusively to talk about the amount of skin covered (or not covered) by a person's clothing. This limitation of the word causes a loss of emphasis on the important virtue of modesty. When mentoring Timothy in his letter, Paul emphasized the importance of living a quiet, peaceful, and dignified life. These are some of the characteristics linked to modesty and are important qualities in the life of a Christian seeking to glorify and bring attention to God rather than self.

First of all, then, I urge that supplications, prayers, intercessions, and thanksgivings be made for all people, for kings and all who are in high positions, that we may lead a peaceful and quiet life, godly and dignified in every way. This is good, and it is pleasing in the sight of God our Savior, who desires all people to be saved and to come to the knowledge of the truth. For there is one God, and there is one mediator between God and men, the man Christ Jesus, who

171

gave himself as a ransom for all, which is the testimony given at the proper time.
I Timothy 2:1-6

Guiding Questions

What person in the Bible, history, literature, or film needed modesty?

When, why, and how should we (or should we NOT) show modesty?

Vices
Modesty can be a virtue in its best and most pure form, but it can quickly become a vice in its extreme form (shyness) or when it is lacking (shamelessness). Continue contemplating modesty by looking at these two misrepresentations of this virtue.

(+) Shyness
Definition: an over realized reluctance of exposing oneself to others; to be timid

Fear not, for I am with you; be not dismayed, for I am your God; I will strengthen you, I will help you, I will uphold you with my righteous right hand.
Isaiah 41:10

(-) Shamelessness
Definition: acting without regard for what is right or wrong

And since they did not see fit to acknowledge God, God gave them up to a debased mind to do what ought not to be done.
Romans 1:28

Guiding Questions

When have you experienced a person being shy or shameless?

What situations cause you to be shy or shameless?

When have you experienced modesty from someone in your life?

How can you cultivate the virtue of modesty in your life?

Circle a number to rate yourself in this virtue:

(-) shamelessness			**Modesty**			shyness (+)		
1	2	3	4	5	4	3	2	1

What kind of person do you want to be?

I am shy when...

I am shameless when...

I am modest when...

I want to be...

Cultivating Virtue

Contemplation #40

(-) in deficiency	**VIRTUE**	(+) in excess
rebellion	**Obedience**	passiveness

"Obedience is an act of faith;
disobedience is the result of unbelief."
Edwin Louis Cole

OBEDIENCE

Definition: acting in compliance with individuals with proper authority over you

We all have someone in life that we must obey and rules and laws we must follow. From the time we are born, obedience is a virtue that we are learning to cultivate, but obedience is oftentimes still difficult for us. We see a good example of the difficulty in balancing this virtue at the very beginning of time. In the garden, Adam and Eve passively obeyed Satan's instructions to eat the forbidden fruit and actively rebelled against God's instructions to refrain from eating of this fruit. Passively following imperfect leaders or rules is as dangerous to our virtue and soul as being rebellious to good instruction.

When the time drew near for David to die, he gave a charge to Solomon his son. "I am about to go the way of all the earth," he said. "So be strong, act like a man, and observe what the Lord your God requires: Walk in obedience to him, and keep his decrees and commands, his laws and regulations, as written in the Law of Moses. Do this so that you may prosper in all you do and wherever you go." I Kings 2:1-3

175

Guiding Questions

What person in the Bible, history, literature, or film needed obedience?

When, why, and how should we (or should we NOT) show obedience?

Vices

Obedience can be a virtue in its best and most pure form, but it can quickly become a vice in its extreme form (passiveness) or when it is lacking (rebellion). Continue contemplating obedience by looking at these two misrepresentations of this virtue.

(+) Passiveness

Definition: not acting on or taking part in personal responsibilities

So whoever knows the right thing to do and fails to do it, for him it is sin.
James 4:17

(-) Rebellion

Definition: actively choosing actions in opposition to one in authority over you

An evil man seeks only rebellion, and a cruel messenger will be sent against him.
Proverbs 17:11

Guiding Questions

When have you experienced a person being passive or rebellious?

What situations cause you to be passive or rebellious?

When have you experienced obedience from someone in your life?

How can you cultivate the virtue of obedience in your life?

Circle a number to rate yourself in this virtue:

(-) rebellion			Obedience			passiveness (+)		
1	2	3	4	5	4	3	2	1

What kind of person do you want to be?

I am passive when...

I am rebellious when...

I am obedient when...

I want to be...

Cultivating Virtue

Contemplation #41

(-) in deficiency	**VIRTUE**	(+) in excess
anxiety	**Optimism**	naivety

"Optimism is the faith that leads to achievement.
Nothing can be done without hope and confidence."
Helen Keller

OPTIMISM

Definition: an inclination to put the most favorable construction upon actions and events or to anticipate the best possible outcome

Optimism comes from hope, but it also inspires hope. A deep and pure understanding and belief in the attributes and actions of God the Father, God the Son, and God the Spirit yields confidence and hope that all things in life will work together for our good. So, even in our darkest hour, we can be optimistic and not fall into the vice of anxiousness. At the same time, we should not be naive to the evils or imperfections around us. As we make plans and take actions, our optimism should also be tempered with wisdom.

The LORD is my light and my salvation; Whom shall I fear?
The LORD is the defense of my life; Whom shall I dread?
When evildoers came upon me to devour my flesh, my
adversaries and my enemies, they stumbled and fell. Though
a host encamp against me, my heart will not fear; Though
war arise against me, in spite of this I shall be confident.
Psalm 27:1-3

Guiding Questions

What person in the Bible, history, literature, or film needed optimism?

When, why, and how should we (or should we NOT) be optimistic?

Vices
Optimism can be a virtue in its best and most pure form, but it can quickly become a vice in its extreme form (naivety) or when it is lacking (anxiety). Continue contemplating optimism by looking at these two misrepresentations of this virtue.

(+) Naivety
Definition: a belief that life is simple and fair, that intentions of people are generally good, and a willingness to believe a person is telling the truth

Brothers, do not be children in your thinking. Be infants in evil, but in your thinking be mature.
I Corinthians 14:20

(-) Anxiety
Definition: extreme uneasiness resulting from fear, worry, or nervousness

And which of you by being anxious can add a single hour to his span of life?
Matthew 6:27

Guiding Questions

When have you experienced a person being naive or anxious?

What situations cause you to be naive or anxious?

When have you experienced optimism from someone in your life?

How can you cultivate the virtue of optimism in your life?

Circle a number to rate yourself in this virtue:

(-) anxiety	Optimism	naivety (+)
1 2 3	4 5 4	3 2 1

What kind of person do you want to be?

I am naive when...

I am anxious when...

I am optimistic when...

I want to be...

Cultivating Virtue

Contemplation #42

(-) in deficiency	VIRTUE	(+) in excess
confusion	Orderliness	nagging

"When loneliness comes stalking, go into the fields, consider the orderliness of the world."
Mary Oliver

ORDERLINESS

Definition: the quality of being well arranged or organized

Our Father in Heaven is the great Creator and a God of order. He is not a nagging micromanager, and He is not the creator of confusion. The desire for order is good; however, we should first focus on the orderliness of our own thoughts and actions before focusing on the orderliness of others. Jesus taught us this basic principal in Matthew 7:5 when He tells us to remove the log of wood from our own eye that is obstructing our vision before seeking to deal with the small piece of wood inhibiting the vision of others around you. Personal orderliness will help guide us to orderliness in our family, church, school, organization, community, state, and nation.

Dress for action like a man; I will question you, and you make it known to me. "Where were you when I laid the foundation of the earth? Tell me, if you have understanding. Who determined its measurements—surely you know! Or who stretched the line upon it? On what were its bases sunk, or who laid its cornerstone, when the morning stars sang together and all the sons of God shouted for joy? Or who shut in the sea with doors when it burst out from the womb, when

I made clouds its garment and thick darkness its swaddling band, and prescribed limits for it and set bars and doors, and said, 'Thus far shall you come, and no farther, and here shall your proud waves be stayed'? Have you commanded the morning since your days began, and caused the dawn to know its place?"
Job 38:3-12

Guiding Questions

What person in the Bible, history, literature, or film needed orderliness?

When, why, and how should we (or should we NOT) be orderly?

Vices

Orderliness can be a virtue in its best and most pure form, but it can quickly become a vice in its extreme form (nagging) or when it is lacking (confusion). Continue contemplating orderliness by looking at these two misrepresentations of this virtue.

(+) Nagging

Definition: constantly harassing someone to do something

Better to live in a dessert than with a quarrelsome and nagging wife. Proverbs 21:19

(-) Confusion

Definition: a lack of understanding or a state of disorder

For God is not a God of confusion but of peace.
I Corinthians 14:33

Guiding Questions

When have you experienced a person nagging or being confusing?

What situations cause you to be nagging or confusing?

When have you experienced orderliness from someone in your life?

How can you cultivate the virtue of orderliness in your life?

Circle a number to rate yourself in this virtue:

(-) confusion	Orderliness	nagging (+)
1 2 3	4 5 4	3 2 1

What kind of person do you want to be?

I am nagging when...

I produce confusion when...

I am orderly when...

I want to be...

185

Cultivating Virtue

Contemplation #43

(-) in deficiency	VIRTUE	(+) in excess
restlessness	Patience*	laziness

"Patience is bitter, but its fruit is sweet."
Aristotle

PATIENCE

Definition: the ability to accept delay, suffering, or annoyance without becoming angry

Patience is not inactivity. James tells us that it is something that we must "be," and Paul tells us in I Corinthians 13 that it is something that love "is." So, impatience can quickly lead to laziness or restlessness if we do not actively pursue and cultivate patience in our hearts and toward others. Patience is also important enough that the Holy Spirit inspired Paul to list it as a fruit of the spirit. Therefore, there is no law against it, and we can never be too patient. This is a difficult concept for modern humans to embrace. Some believe that impatience and restlessness are virtues because we should expect quick service and that quickness is the result of excellent productivity. Look for ways to push against this in your life today because patience truly is a virtue.

Be patient, therefore, brothers, until the coming of the Lord. See how the farmer waits for the precious fruit of the earth, being patient about it, until it receives the early and the late rains. You also, be patient. Establish your hearts, for the coming of the Lord is at hand. Do not grumble against one another, brothers, so that you may not be judged;

behold, the Judge is standing at the door. As an example of suffering and patience, brothers, take the prophets who spoke in the name of the Lord. Behold, we consider those blessed who remained steadfast.
James 5:7-11

Guiding Questions

What person in the Bible, history, literature, or film needed patience?

When, why, and how should we (or should we NOT) be patient?

Vices

Patience can be a virtue in its best and most pure form, but it can quickly become a vice in its extreme form (laziness) or when it is lacking (restlessness). Continue contemplating patience by looking at these two misrepresentations of this virtue.

(+) Laziness

Definition: not willing to work or put forth any effort

The desire of the lazy man kills him, for his hands refuse to labor.
Ephesians 4:31

(-) Restlessness

Definition: being unwilling to stay still or to be quiet and calm due to being worried or bored

When you work the ground, it will no longer yield its crops for you. You will be a restless wanderer on the earth.
Proverbs 29:8

Guiding Questions

When have you experienced a person being lazy or restless?

What situations cause you to be lazy or restless?

When have you experienced patience from someone in your life?

How can you cultivate the virtue of patience in your life?

Circle a number to rate yourself in this virtue:

(-) restlessness	Patience*		laziness (+)
1 2 3	4 5 4		3 2 1

What kind of person do you want to be?

I am lazy when...

I am restless when...

I am patient when...

I want to be...

Cultivating Virtue

Contemplation #44

(-) in deficiency	VIRTUE	(+) in excess
anxiety	Peace*	impotence

"A mind at peace does not engender wars."
Sophocles

PEACE

Definition: calm, quiet, and free from worry or annoyance

Jesus came down to earth from heaven to bring us peace. This is not simply a shallow peace and calm that just touches the surface. True peace is so much deeper and more sustaining than an exterior expression of calm. I like to picture Jesus saying to the waves and storms of our lives, "Peace, be still," just as He spoke to the waves and storm at the Sea of Galilee. I do not imagine that it was just the waves and sky that became calm that day. I believe that the teeming turmoil of sea creatures and the entire unseen marine ecosystem also became calm in that moment that Jesus spoke. This is the virtue of deep peace that we must pursue, express, and accept from God each day.

Repay no one evil for evil, but give thought to do what is honorable in the sight of all. If possible, so far as it depends on you, live peaceably with all. Beloved, never avenge yourselves, but leave it to the wrath of God, for it is written, "Vengeance is mine, I will repay, says the Lord." To the contrary, "if your enemy is hungry, feed him; if he is thirsty, give him something to drink; for by so doing you will heap

191

burning coals on his head." Do not be overcome by evil, but overcome evil with good.
Romans 12:17-21

Guiding Questions

What person in the Bible, history, literature, or film needed peace?

When, why, and how should we (or should we NOT) be peaceful?

Vices
Peace can be a virtue in its best and most pure form, but it can quickly become a vice in its extreme form (impotence) or when it is lacking (anxiety). Continue contemplating peace by looking at these two misrepresentations of this virtue.

(+) Impotence
Definition: lacking the power, ability, or desire to change, improve, or react to a situation

Watch and pray so that you will not fall into temptation. The spirit is willing, but the flesh is weak.
Matthew 26:41

(-) Anxiety
Definition: extreme uneasiness resulting from fear, worry, or nervousness

Do not be anxious about anything, but in everything by prayer and supplication with thanksgiving let your requests be made known to God. And the peace of God, which

surpasses all understanding, will guard your hearts and your minds in Christ Jesus.
Philippians 4:6-7

Guiding Questions

When have you experienced a person being impotent or anxious?

What situations cause you to be impotent or anxious?

When have you experienced peace from someone in your life?

How can you cultivate the virtue of peace in your life?

Circle a number to rate yourself in this virtue:

(-) anxiety			Peace*			impotence (+)		
1	2	3	4	5	4	3	2	1

What kind of person do you want to be?

I am impotent when...

I am anxious when...

I am at peace when...

I want to be...

193

Cultivating Virtue

Contemplation #45

(-) in deficiency	**VIRTUE**	(+) in excess
negligence	**Pensiveness**	criticalness

*"Let those who thoughtfully
consider the brevity of life remember
the length of eternity."*
Thomas Ken

PENSIVENESS

Definition: quietly thinking about deep or serious issues

David's writings in Psalm 23 are a comfort to many individuals struggling with sadness and loss experienced in life. However, this passage of Scripture also teaches us to be pensive. Our high-paced society often favors speed over thoroughness and emotional reactions over thoughtful reason. When brought to a point of balance in life, creating space in your life to be pensive is an important aspect of achieving the good life. Find time and space to quietly think about important, philosophical, and religious issues.

The Lord is my shepherd; I shall not want. He makes me lie down in green pastures. He leads me beside still waters. He restores my soul. He leads me in paths of righteousness for his name's sake. Even though I walk through the valley of the shadow of death, I will fear no evil, for you are with me; your rod and your staff, they comfort me. You prepare a table before me in the presence of my enemies; you anoint my head with oil; my cup overflows. Surely goodness and mercy

195

shall follow me all the days of my life, and I shall dwell in the house of the LORD forever.
Psalm 23:1-6

Guiding Questions

What person in the Bible, history, literature, or film needed to be pensive?

When, why, and how should we (or should we NOT) be pensive?

Vices

Pensiveness can be a virtue in its best and most pure form, but it can quickly become a vice in its extreme form (criticalness) or when it is lacking (negligence). Continue contemplating pensiveness by looking at these two misrepresentations of this virtue.

(+) Criticalness

Definition: expressing a negative opinion about someone or something

Let no corrupting talk come out of your mouths, but only such as is good for building up, as fits the occasion, that it may give grace to those who hear.
Ephesians 4:29

(-) Negligence

Definition: not being careful or giving enough attention to people or things that are your responsibility

My sons, do not now be negligent, for the Lord has chosen you to stand in his presence, to minister to him and to be his ministers and make offerings to him.
II Chronicles 29:11

Guiding Questions

When have you experienced a person being critical or negligent?

What situations cause you to be critical or negligent?

When have you experienced pensiveness from someone in your life?

How can you cultivate the virtue of pensiveness in your life?

Circle a number to rate yourself in this virtue:

(-) negligence			Pensiveness			criticalness (+)		
1	2	3	4	5	4	3	2	1

What kind of person do you want to be?

I am critical when...

I am negligent when...

I am pensive when...

I want to be...

197

Cultivating Virtue

Contemplation #46

(-) in deficiency	**VIRTUE**	(+) in excess
passiveness	**Perseverance**	arrogance

"Many of life's failures are people who did not realize how close they were to success when they gave up."
Thomas Edison

PERSEVERANCE

Definition: continued effort and determination in spite of difficulties or setbacks

There are some things in life that you will not and cannot achieve. However, many of your desires are achievable and you need to find a way to cultivate the will to accomplish them. Perseverance is a virtue that is easy to neglect. Setbacks are hard and difficulties are frustrating, but perseverance results from rightly ordered faith, hope, and love.

More than that, we rejoice in our sufferings, knowing that suffering produces endurance, and endurance produces character, and character produces hope, and hope does not put us to shame, because God's love has been poured into our hearts through the Holy Spirit who has been given to us.
Romans 5:3-5

Guiding Questions

What person in the Bible, history, literature, or film needed perseverance?

199

When, why, and how should we (or should we NOT) persevere?

Vices
Perseverance can be a virtue in its best and most pure form, but it can quickly become a vice in its extreme form (arrogance) or when it is lacking (passiveness). Continue contemplating perseverance by looking at these two misrepresentations of this virtue.

(+) Arrogance
Definition: proud in an unpleasant way and behaving as if you are better or more important than other people

"Scoffer" is the name of the arrogant, haughty man who acts with arrogant pride.
Proverbs 21:24

(-) Passiveness
Definition: not reacting or engaging in a situation

Speak up for those who cannot speak for themselves, for the rights of all who are destitute. Speak up and judge fairly; defend the rights of the poor and needy.
Proverbs 31:8-9

Guiding Questions

When have you experienced a person being arrogant or passive?

What situations cause you to be arrogant or passive?

When have you experienced perseverance from someone in your life?

How can you cultivate the virtue of perseverance in your life?

Circle a number to rate yourself in this virtue:

(-) passiveness			Perseverance			arrogance (+)		
1	2	3	4	5	4	3	2	1

What kind of person do you want to be?

I am arrogant when...

I am passive when...

I show perseverance when...

I want to be...

Cultivating Virtue

Contemplation #47

(-) in deficiency	**VIRTUE**	(+) in excess
apathy	**Purposefulness**	worry

"The person without a purpose
is like a ship without a rudder."
Thomas Carlyle

PURPOSEFULNESS

Definition: a determined aim at achieving a goal

Theologians gathered together in London, England, in the mid-1600's to clarify and document their understanding of the Bible and the Christian faith. Their efforts produced the Westminster Confession of Faith and Catechism. The first question of this document seeks to clarify our primary purpose in life. First Corinthians 10:31 teaches that our primary purpose in life is to glorify God. Everything else we do in life should be purposefully in line with this main purpose. The virtue of purposefulness gives meaning to life.

"You are the salt of the earth, but if salt has lost its taste, how shall its saltiness be restored? It is no longer good for anything except to be thrown out and trampled under people's feet. "You are the light of the world. A city set on a hill cannot be hidden. Nor do people light a lamp and put it under a basket, but on a stand, and it gives light to all in the house. In the same way, let your light shine before others, so that they may see your good works and give glory to your Father who is in heaven.
Matthew 5:13-16

Guiding Questions

What person in the Bible, history, literature, or film needed to be purposeful?

When, why, and how should we (or should we NOT) be purposeful?

Vices

Purposefulness can be a virtue in its best and most pure form, but it can quickly become a vice in its extreme form (worry) or when it is lacking (apathy). Continue contemplating purposefulness by looking at these two misrepresentations of this virtue.

(+) Worry

Definition: to think about unpleasant things or possible problems that could distract from accomplishing something

Cast all your anxiety on him because he cares for you.
I Peter 5:7

(-) Apathy

Definition: a lack of interest of care toward a person or thing

Because I have heard of your faith in the Lord Jesus and your love toward all the saints, I do not cease to give thanks for you, remembering you in my prayers.
Ephesians 1:15-16

Guiding Questions

When have you experienced a person being worrisome or apathetic?

What situations cause you to be worrisome or apathetic?

When have you experienced purposefulness from someone in your life?

How can you cultivate the virtue of purposefulness in your life?

Circle a number to rate yourself in this virtue:

(-) apathy			Purposefulness			worry (+)		
1	2	3	4	5	4	3	2	1

What kind of person do you want to be?

I worry when...

I am apathetic when...

I am purposeful when...

I want to be...

Cultivating Virtue

Contemplation #48

(-) in deficiency	VIRTUE	(+) in excess
disregard	**Respect**	idolatry

"When we love and respect people,
revealing to them their value, they can begin to
come out from behind the walls that protect them."
Jean Vanier

RESPECT

Definition: a polite attitude shown toward someone or something that you consider important

The definition of respect listed above seems to imply that you should only show respect for individuals who you consider important. However, as you develop the virtues of humility and dignity, you will realize that respect is the golden mean between holding a person too highly (idolatry) and treating others as subhuman (disregard). You must also acknowledge and respect yourself rightly between these two vices.

Let every person be subject to the governing authorities.
For there is no authority except from God, and those that
exist have been instituted by God. Therefore, whoever resists
the authorities resists what God has appointed, and those
who resist will incur judgment. For rulers are not a terror to
good conduct, but to bad. Would you have no fear of the one
who is in authority? Then do what is good, and you will
receive his approval, for he is God's servant for your good.
But if you do wrong, be afraid, for he does not bear the sword
in vain. For he is the servant of God, an avenger who carries

out God's wrath on the wrongdoer. Therefore, one must be in subjection, not only to avoid God's wrath but also for the sake of conscience.
Romans 13:1-5

Guiding Questions

What person in the Bible, history, literature, or film needed respect?

When, why, and how should we (or should we NOT) be respectful?

Vices
Respect can be a virtue in its best and most pure form, but it can quickly become a vice in its extreme form (idolatry) or when it is lacking (disregard). Continue contemplating respect by looking at these two misrepresentations of this virtue.

(+) Idolatry
Definition: an immodest attachment of devotion, loyalty, or worship of someone or something

Therefore, my beloved, flee from idolatry.
I Corinthians 1:15

(-) Disregard
Definition: a lack of consideration for someone or something

Let each of you look not only to his own interests, but also to the interests of others.
Philippians 2:4

Guiding Questions

When have you experienced a person being idolatrous or disregarding?

What situations cause you to be idolatrous or disregarding?

When have you experienced respect from someone in your life?

How can you cultivate the virtue of respect in your life?

Circle a number to rate yourself in this virtue:

(-) disregard			Respect			idolatry (+)		
1	2	3	4	5	4	3	2	1

What kind of person do you want to be?

I show idolatry when...

I show disregard when...

I am respectful when...

I want to be...

Cultivating Virtue

Contemplation #49

(-) in deficiency	**VIRTUE**	(+) in excess
unreliability	**Responsibility**	workaholism

"Action springs not from thought,
but from a readiness for responsibility."
Dietrich Bonhoeffer

RESPONSIBILITY

Definition: good judgment and the ability to act and make good decisions

Responsibility is an important aspect of a meaningful life, the good life, and a life well lived. Responsibility was one of the first things granted to humanity after being created. At the end of Genesis 1, God gave Adam and Eve the responsibilities to reproduce and to care for the earth and animals. Responsibility is a helpful gift that gives practical meaning to life. Do not avoid responsibility. Look for ways that you or your children can cultivate and embrace responsibility.

"For it will be like a man going on a journey, who called his servants and entrusted to them his property. To one he gave five talents, to another two, to another one, to each according to his ability. Then he went away. He who had received the five talents went at once and traded with them, and he made five talents more. So also he who had the two talents made two talents more. But he who had received the one talent went and dug in the ground and hid his master's money. Now after a long time the master of those servants came and settled accounts with them. And he who had

211

received the five talents came forward, bringing five talents more, saying, 'Master, you delivered to me five talents; here, I have made five talents more.' His master said to him, 'Well done, good and faithful servant. You have been faithful over a little; I will set you over much. Enter into the joy of your master.'"
Matthew 25:14-21

Guiding Questions

What person in the Bible, history, literature, or film needed responsibility?

When, why, and how should we (or should we NOT) be responsible?

Vices

Responsibility can be a virtue in its best and most pure form, but it can quickly become a vice in its extreme form (workaholism) or when it is lacking (unreliability). Continue contemplating responsibility by looking at these two misrepresentations of this virtue.

(+) Workaholism

Definition: a person who spends too much time working and finds it difficult not to work

Do not toil to acquire wealth; be discerning enough to desist.
Proverbs 23:4

(-) Unreliability

Definition: not able to be trusted or believed

For many will come in My name, saying 'I am the Christ,' and will mislead many.
Matthew 24:5

Guiding Questions

When have you experienced a person being a workaholic or unreliable?

What situations cause you to be a workaholic or unreliable?

When have you experienced responsibility from someone in your life?

How can you cultivate the virtue of responsibility in your life?

Circle a number to rate yourself in this virtue:

(-) unreliability			Responsibility			workaholism (+)		
1	2	3	4	5	4	3	2	1

What kind of person do you want to be?

I am a workaholic when...

I am unreliable when...

I am responsible when...

I want to be...

213

Cultivating Virtue

Contemplation #50

(-) in deficiency	**VIRTUE**	(+) in excess
wastefulness	**Resourcefulness**	stinginess

"If necessity is the mother of invention,
then resourcefulness is the father."
Beulah Louise Henry

RESOURCEFULNESS

Definition: the ability to make decisions or to act on your own
to make the most of limited opportunities or resources

Developing the virtue of resourcefulness will also help us to
cultivate industriousness, perseverance, and joy. One of the
best places to start looking at the virtue of resourcefulness in
your own life is to look closely at your budget. Track every
dollar you spend for the next three months. Are you generous
to others or wastefully inclined toward spending money on
self-pleasure? Being resourceful requires living a little
differently than others, but it can be a fun "game" to look for
the best deals or to make personal belongings last longer
before replacing them.

An excellent wife who can find? She is far more precious
than jewels. The heart of her husband trusts in her, and he
will have no lack of gain. She does him good, and not harm,
all the days of her life. She seeks wool and flax, and works
with willing hands. She is like the ships of the merchant; she
brings her food from afar. She rises while it is yet night
and provides food for her household and portions for her
maidens. She considers a field and buys it; with the fruit of

her hands she plants a vineyard. She dresses herself with strength and makes her arms strong. She perceives that her merchandise is profitable. Her lamp does not go out at night. She puts her hands to the distaff, and her hands hold the spindle. She opens her hand to the poor and reaches out her hands to the needy. She is not afraid of snow for her household, for all her household are clothed in scarlet. She makes bed coverings for herself; her clothing is fine linen and purple. Her husband is known in the gates when he sits among the elders of the land. She makes linen garments and sells them; she delivers sashes to the merchant. Strength and dignity are her clothing, and she laughs at times to come.
Proverbs 31:10-25

Guiding Questions

What person in the Bible, history, literature, or film needed to be resourceful?

When, why, and how should we (or should we NOT) be resourceful?

Vices

Resourcefulness can be a virtue in its best and most pure form, but it can quickly become a vice in its extreme form (stinginess) or when it is lacking (wastefulness). Continue contemplating resourcefulness by looking at these two misrepresentations of this virtue.

(+) Stinginess

Definition: unwillingness to spend money or share your possessions or talents with others

A stingy man hastens after wealth and does not know that poverty will come upon him.
Proverbs 28:22

(-) Wastefulness
Definition: using something in a careless and thoughtless way that produces far less than optimal results

Precious treasure and oil are in a wise man's dwelling, but a foolish man devours it.
Proverbs 21:20

Guiding Questions

When have you experienced a person being stingy or wasteful?

What situations cause you to be stingy or wasteful?

When have you experienced resourcefulness from someone in your life?

How can you cultivate the virtue of resourcefulness in your life?

Circle a number to rate yourself in this virtue:

(-) wastefulness	Resourcefulness	stinginess (+)
1 2 3	4 5 4	3 2 1

What kind of person do you want to be?

I am stingy when...

I am wasteful when...

I am resourceful when...

I want to be...

Cultivating Virtue

Contemplation #51

(-) in deficiency	VIRTUE	(+) in excess
irreverence	**Righteousness**	haughtiness

"We do not become righteous by doing righteous deeds but,
having been made righteous, we do righteous deeds."
Martin Luther

RIGHTEOUSNESS

Definition: behaving in a morally correct way

Righteousness encompasses most of the other virtues. As Christians, we know that we became completely unrighteous when Adam sinned in the Garden of Eden. However, we are seen as fully righteous through the perfect life, death, and resurrection of Jesus. This tension of being made righteous by Christ yet not yet being perfected here on earth is the reason we must actively study and work to develop a virtuous life. As Paul wrote in Romans 7, there are so many times that we do not do what we want to do, and we do what we do not want to do. This is the daily struggle of living a righteous life.

He who walks righteously and speaks uprightly, who despises the gain of oppressions, who shakes his hands, lest they hold a bribe, who stops his ears from hearing of bloodshed and shuts his eyes from looking on evil, he will dwell on the heights; his place of defense will be the fortresses of rocks; his bread will be given him; his water will be sure. Your eyes will behold the king in his beauty; they will see a land that stretches afar.
Matthew 25:19-28

219

Guiding Questions

What person in the Bible, history, literature, or film needed to be righteous?

When, why, and how should we (or should we NOT) be righteous?

Vices

Righteousness can be a virtue in its best and most pure form, but it can quickly become a vice in its extreme form (haughtiness) or when it is lacking (irreverence). Continue contemplating righteousness by looking at these two misrepresentations of this virtue.

(+) Haughtiness

Definition: unreasonably proud from a belief that you are better than other people

To do righteousness and justice is more acceptable to the Lord than sacrifice. Haughty eyes and a proud heart, the lamp of the wicked, are sin.
Proverbs 21:3-4

(-) Irreverence

Definition: not showing a proper respect for important, honorable, or holy things

Let the lying lips be mute, which speak arrogantly against the righteous with pride and contempt.
Psalms 31:18

Guiding Questions

When have you experienced a person being haughty or irreverent?

What situations cause you to be haughty or irreverent?

When have you experienced righteousness from someone in your life?

How can you cultivate the virtue of righteousness in your life?

Circle a number to rate yourself in this virtue:

(-) irreverence	Righteousness	haughtiness (+)
1 2 3	4 5 4	3 2 1

What kind of person do you want to be?

I am haughty when...

I am irreverent when...

I show righteousness when...

I want to be...

Cultivating Virtue

Contemplation #52

(-) in deficiency	VIRTUE	(+) in excess
wildness	Self-Control*	stoicism

"What lies in our power to do,
it lies in our power not to do."
Aristotle

SELF-CONTROL

Definition: the ability to manage your emotions, thoughts, and actions in an intentionally restrained manner for the good of others and the glory of God

Self-control is important in the development and practice of many other virtues. If you have ever played a sport or watched a sporting event, you can appreciate Paul's analogy of self-control in I Corinthians 9 to developing as an athlete. Self-control requires the discipline of habits, thoughts, desires, and actions. Almost everything in our lives is influenced by, or the result of, our self-control. Be careful, however, not to fall into the vice of excess which results in being stoically unemotional and inactive.

Do you not know that in a race all the runners run, but only one receives the prize? So run that you may obtain it. Every athlete exercises self-control in all things. They do it to receive a perishable wreath, but we an imperishable. So I do not run aimlessly; I do not box as one beating the air. But I discipline my body and keep it under control, lest after preaching to others I myself should be disqualified.
I Corinthians 9:24-27

223

Guiding Questions

What person in the Bible, history, literature, or film needed self-control?

When, why, and how should we (or should we NOT) be self-controlled?

Vices

Self-control can be a virtue in its best and most pure form, but it can quickly become a vice in its extreme form (stoicism) or when it is lacking (wildness). Continue contemplating self-control by looking at these two misrepresentations of this virtue.

(+) Stoicism

Definition: not showing any feeling or emotion

Jesus wept. So, the Jews said, "See how he loved him!"
John 11:35-36

(-) Wildness

Definition: expressing extreme and uncontrolled emotions

A fool gives full vent to his spirit, but a wise man quietly holds it back.
Proverbs 29:11

Guiding Questions

When have you experienced a person being stoic or wild?

What situations cause you to be stoic or wild?

When have you experienced self-control from someone in your life?

How can you cultivate the virtue of self-control in your life?

Circle a number to rate yourself in this virtue:

(-) wildness			Self-Control*			stoicism (+)		
1	2	3	4	5	4	3	2	1

What kind of person do you want to be?

I am stoic when...

I am wild when...

I show self-control when...

I want to be...

Cultivating Virtue

Contemplation #53

(-) in deficiency	**VIRTUE**	(+) in excess
unfeeling	**Sensitivity**	anxiety

"Manners are a sensitive awareness
of the feelings of others."
Emily Post

SENSITIVITY

Definition: a special awareness and understanding of other people's feelings and needs

Jesus summarized the Old Testament law by commanding us to love God and love others. The complete fulfillment of both commands requires the virtue of sensitivity. Sensitivity requires us to be open to the Holy Spirit and open to the beliefs, feelings, and past experiences of others. This necessitates the virtues of empathy, servanthood, humility, and kindness.

For if a man wearing a gold ring and fine clothing comes into your assembly, and a poor man in shabby clothing also comes in, and if you pay attention to the one who wears the fine clothing and say, "You sit here in a good place," while you say to the poor man, "You stand over there," or, "Sit down at my feet," have you not then made distinctions among yourselves and become judges with evil thoughts? Listen, my beloved brothers, has not God chosen those who are poor in the world to be rich in faith and heirs of the kingdom, which he has promised to those who love him?
James 2:2-5

Guiding Questions

What person in the Bible, history, literature, or film needed to be sensitive?

When, why, and how should we (or should we NOT) be sensitive?

Vices
Sensitivity can be a virtue in its best and most pure form, but it can quickly become a vice in its extreme form (anxiety) or when it is lacking (unfeeling). Continue contemplating sensitivity by looking at these two misrepresentations of this virtue.

(+) Anxiety
Definition: becoming preoccupied with worry, fear, or nervousness over something you cannot control

But Martha was distracted with much serving. And she went up to him and said, "Lord, do you not care that my sister has left me to serve alone? Tell her then to help me." But the Lord answered her, "Martha, Martha, you are anxious and troubled about many things, but one thing is necessary. Mary has chosen the good portion, which will not be taken away from her."
Luke 10:40-42

(-) Unfeeling
Definition: having no sympathy for the suffering or concerns of other people

Keep your heart with all vigilance, for from it flow the springs of life.
Proverbs 4:23

Guiding Questions

When have you experienced a person being anxious or unfeeling?

What situations cause you to be anxious or unfeeling?

When have you experienced sensitivity from someone in your life?

How can you cultivate the virtue of sensitivity in your life?

Circle a number to rate yourself in this virtue:

(-) unfeeling	Sensitivity	anxiety (+)
1 2 3	4 5 4	3 2 1

What kind of person do you want to be?

I am anxious when...

I am unfeeling when...

I am sensitive to other when...

I want to be...

Cultivating Virtue

Contemplation #54

(-) in deficiency	VIRTUE	(+) in excess
inconsideration	**Servanthood**	slavery

"The measure of a man's greatness is not the number of servants he has, but the number of people he serves."
John Hagee

SERVANTHOOD

Definition: taking action to use your knowledge, abilities, or resources to help and care for other people in a way that might not benefit you

The entire Christian life is one of service. This may be a tough concept to fully process and live out, but we are called to serve God through a life seeking to glorify Him. This is why Jesus gave us, his servants, the command to love God and others. A life of service, however, should not cause us to think of human examples of American slavery or ancient Greek servants of imperfect masters. Our servanthood is called out of us by God's love for us and our resulting love for Him.

But Jesus called them to him and said, "You know that the rulers of the Gentiles lord it over them, and their great ones exercise authority over them. It shall not be so among you. But whoever would be great among you must be your servant, and whoever would be first among you must be your slave, even as the Son of Man came not to be served but to serve, and to give his life as a ransom for many."
Matthew 20:25-28

231

Guiding Questions

What person in the Bible, history, literature, or film needed servanthood?

When, why, and how should we (or should we NOT) be servants?

Vices

Servanthood can be a virtue in its best and most pure form, but it can quickly become a vice in its extreme form (slavery) or when it is lacking (inconsideration). Continue contemplating servanthood by looking at these two misrepresentations of this virtue.

(+) Slavery

Definition: taking action after being compelled by force, guilt, or coercion

The rich rules over the poor, and the borrower is the slave of the lender.
Proverbs 22:7

(-) Inconsideration

Definition: not caring about the feelings or needs of others

Let no one seek his own good, but the good of his neighbor.
I Corinthians 10:24

Guiding Questions

When have you experienced a person being a slave or inconsiderate?

What situations cause you to be slave or inconsiderate?

When have you experienced servanthood from someone in your life?

How can you cultivate the virtue of servanthood in your life?

Circle a number to rate yourself in this virtue:

(-) inconsideration			Servanthood			slavery (+)	
1	2	3	4	5	4	3	2	1

What kind of person do you want to be?

I am a slave when...

I am inconsiderate when...

I am a servant when...

I want to be...

Cultivating Virtue

Contemplation #55

(-) in deficiency	VIRTUE	(+) in excess
stubbornness	**Teachability**	naivety

*"Intellectual growth should commence
at birth and cease only at death."*
Albert Einstein

TEACHABILITY

Definition: the desire and ability to learn and change

The idea of being a lifelong learner is commonly talked about in education, but we often have areas of our life that we believe we have mastered and need no further growth of guidance from others. This stubborn, naive, and prideful attitude prevents us from being teachable and stunts our growth. Are there ways that you can be more teachable in your life? Experience is also a good teacher, but you must be open to learning for it to be effective.

The proverbs of Solomon, son of David, king of Israel: To know wisdom and instruction, to understand words of insight, to receive instruction in wise dealing, in righteousness, justice, and equity; to give prudence to the simple, knowledge and discretion to the youth— Let the wise hear and increase in learning, and the one who understands obtain guidance, to understand a proverb and a saying, the words of the wise and their riddles. The fear of the Lord is the beginning of knowledge; fools despise wisdom and instruction.
Proverbs 1:1-7

Guiding Questions

What person in the Bible, history, literature, or film needed to be teachable?

When, why, and how should we (or should we NOT) be teachable?

Vices

Teachability can be a virtue in its best and most pure form, but it can quickly become a vice in its extreme form (naivety) or when it is lacking (stubbornness). Continue contemplating teachability by looking at these two misrepresentations of this virtue.

(+) Naivety

Definition: too readily believing someone or something without reason or experience

I appeal to you, brothers, to watch out for those who cause divisions and create obstacles contrary to the doctrine that you have been taught; avoid them. For such persons do not serve our Lord Christ, but their own appetites, and by smooth talk and flattery they deceive the hearts of the naive.
Romans 16:17-18

(+) Stubbornness

Definition: having or showing dogged determination not to change one's attitude or position on something, especially in spite of good arguments or reasons to do so

Poverty and disgrace come to him who ignores instruction, but whoever heeds reproof is honored.
Proverbs 13:18

Guiding Questions

When have you experienced a person being naive or stubborn?

What situations cause you to be naive or stubborn?

When have you experienced teachability from someone in your life?

How can you cultivate the virtue of teachability in your life?

Circle a number to rate yourself in this virtue:

(-) stubbornness		Teachability		naivety (+)	
1	2	3	4	5	4	3	2	1

What kind of person do you want to be?

I am naive when...

I am stubborn when...

I am teachable when...

I want to be...

Cultivating Virtue

Contemplation #56

(-) in deficiency	**VIRTUE**	(+) in excess
carelessness	**Thoughtfulness**	withdrawn

"Did you ever stop to think, and forget to start again?"
Winnie the Pooh

THOUGHTFULNESS

Definition: thinking seriously about ideas and considering the consequences of possible actions based on the ideas being considered

Taking time to stop and think is often difficult is our high-paced modern society. Developing the virtue of thoughtfulness might require you to make several intentional changes in your current habits. The "noise" of constantly being connected to others via text messaging, social media, and increased metropolitan living crowds out the time and space we need to be thoughtful. Through self-examination, you can find and create more opportunities to be thoughtful.

Now therefore, thus says the LORD of hosts, "Consider your ways! "You have sown much, but harvest little; you eat, but there is not enough to be satisfied; you drink, but there is not enough to become drunk; you put on clothing, but no one is warm enough; and he who earns, earns wages to put into a purse with holes." "Thus says the Lord of hosts: Consider your ways. Go up to the hills and bring wood and build the house, that I may take pleasure in it and that I may be glorified," says the Lord.
Haggai 1:5-7

Guiding Questions

What person in the Bible, history, literature, or film needed to be thoughtful?

When, why, and how should we (or should we NOT) be thoughtful?

Vices
Thoughtfulness can be a virtue in its best and most pure form, but it can quickly become a vice in its extreme form (withdrawn) or when it is lacking (carelessness). Continue contemplating thoughtfulness by looking at these two misrepresentations of this virtue.

(+) Withdrawn
Definition: preferring to be alone and taking little interest in other people

Two are better than one, because they have a good return for their labor.
Ecclesiastes 4:9

(-) Carelessness
Definition: acting recklessly as the result of poor planning or limited consideration of possible consequences

But test everything; hold fast what is good.
I Thessalonians 5:21

Guiding Questions

When have you experienced a person being withdrawn or careless?

What situations cause you to be withdrawn or careless?

When have you experienced thoughtfulness from someone in your life?

How can you cultivate the virtue of thoughtfulness in your life?

Circle a number to rate yourself in this virtue:

(-) carelessness	**Thoughtfulness**	withdrawn (+)
1 2 3	4 5 4	3 2 1

What kind of person do you want to be?

I am withdrawn when...

I am careless when...

I am thoughtful when...

I want to be...

Cultivating Virtue

Contemplation #57

(-) in deficiency	**VIRTUE**	(+) in excess
prejudice	**Tolerance**	licentiousness

"Tolerance is giving to every other human being
every right that you claim for yourself."
Robert Green Ingersoll

TOLERANCE

Definition: willing to accept behavior or beliefs that are different from your own but do not violate fundamental morals, ethics, or commands from Scripture

The modern concept of tolerance evokes strong political and moral feelings involving polarizing ideas of gender, marriage, and more. However, the classic understanding of tolerance involves more minor day-to-day interactions. As noted in the definition above, tolerance does not require you to accept immoral ideas or behavior that go against God's Word. Tolerance involves patience, kindness, and calmness when you encounter people that act in ways that are different or annoying to you and your preferences.

As for the one who is weak in faith, welcome him, but not to quarrel over opinions. One person believes he may eat anything, while the weak person eats only vegetables. Let not the one who eats despise the one who abstains, and let not the one who abstains pass judgment on the one who eats, for God has welcomed him. Who are you to pass judgment on the servant of another? It is before his own master that he

*stands or falls. And he will be upheld, for the Lord is able to
make him stand.*
Romans 14:1-4

Guiding Questions

What person in the Bible, history, literature, or film needed
tolerance?

When, why, and how should we (or should we NOT) be
tolerant?

Vices

Tolerance can be a virtue in its best and most pure form, but
it can quickly become a vice in its extreme form
(licentiousness) or when it is lacking (prejudice). Continue
contemplating tolerance by looking at these two
misrepresentations of this virtue.

(+) Licentiousness

Definition: behavior that seeks self-pleasure but goes against
morality and ethics

*They, having become callous, have given themselves over to
sensuality for the practice of every kind of impurity with
greediness.*
Ephesians 4:19

(-) Prejudice

Definition: unfair and unreasonable opinions or feelings
formed without enough information or knowledge

*Do not judge by appearances, but judge with right
judgment."*
John 7:24

Guiding Questions

When have you experienced a person being licentious or prejudiced?

What situations cause you to be licentious or prejudiced?

When have you experienced tolerance from someone in your life?

How can you cultivate the virtue of tolerance in your life?

Circle a number to rate yourself in this virtue:

(-) prejudice			Tolerance			licentiousness (+)		
1	2	3	4	5	4	3	2	1

What kind of person do you want to be?

I am licentious when...

I show prejudice when...

I am tolerant when...

I want to be...

Cultivating Virtue

Contemplation #58

(-) in deficiency	VIRTUE	(+) in excess
deception	**Truthfulness**	rudeness

"A man that seeks truth and loves it must be reckoned precious to any human society."
Epictetus

TRUTHFULNESS

Definition: being honest and not lying in the way you talk, act, and think

Truthfulness involves more than just the words that we say. It also requires us to take actions that will cause others to understand our true motives and desired outcome. This is scary. We do not always want other people to know us that intimately because our motives and desires are not always pure. The virtue of truthfulness also involves thinking truthfully about ourselves and others rather than seeking to convince ourselves of wrong ideas. Seek to uncover subtle patterns of deception or rudeness in your life and find ways to move toward the golden mean of truthfulness.

Then Pilate said to him, "So you are a king?" Jesus answered, "You say that I am a king. For this purpose I was born and for this purpose I have come into the world—to bear witness to the truth. Everyone who is of the truth listens to my voice." Pilate said to him, "What is truth?" After he had said this, he went back outside to the Jews and told them, "I find no guilt in him"
John 8:37-38

247

Guiding Questions

What person in the Bible, history, literature, or film needed to be truthful?

When, why, and how should we (or should we NOT) be truthful?

Vices
Truthfulness can be a virtue in its best and most pure form, but it can quickly become a vice in its extreme form (rudeness) or when it is lacking (deception). Continue contemplating truthfulness by looking at these two misrepresentations of this virtue.

(+) Rudeness
Definition: being offensive or not polite

A soft answer turns away wrath, but a harsh word stirs up anger.
Proverbs 15:1

(-) Deception
Definition: a statement or action that hides the truth and leads other to think wrongly

You are of your father the devil, and your will is to do your father's desires. He was a murderer from the beginning, and has nothing to do with the truth, because there is no truth in him. When he lies, he speaks out of his own character, for he is a liar and the father of lies.
John 8:44

Guiding Questions

When have you experienced a person being rude or deceptive?

What situations cause you to be rude or deceptive?

When have you experienced truthfulness from someone in your life?

How can you cultivate the virtue of truthfulness in your life?

Circle a number to rate yourself in this virtue:

(-) deception			Truthfulness			rudeness (+)		
1	2	3	4	5	4	3	2	1

What kind of person do you want to be?

I am rude when...

I am deceptive when...

I am truthful when...

I want to be...

Cultivating Virtue

Contemplation #59

(-) in deficiency	VIRTUE	(+) in excess
ignorance	**Wisdom**	disdain

"When anger enters the mind, wisdom departs."
Thomas A Kempis

WISDOM

Definition: the ability to use your knowledge, belief, and experience to make good decisions or give good advice

Some ancient philosophers believed that wisdom was the root of all other virtues, but we read in Scripture that there is something that comes before wisdom. Proverbs 9:10 and Psalm 111:10 teach us that "the fear of the LORD is the beginning of wisdom." This "fear" is a respect and awe of who He is and for His attributes and characteristics that set Him apart from humanity. There are many great portions of Scripture about wisdom and the importance of cultivating wisdom in our lives. The well-balanced virtue of wisdom in your life should lead to understanding and rightly ordered actions as you seek to glorify God and enjoy Him forever.

Who is wise and understanding among you? By his good conduct let him show his works in the meekness of wisdom. But if you have bitter jealousy and selfish ambition in your hearts, do not boast and be false to the truth. This is not the wisdom that comes down from above, but is earthly, unspiritual, demonic. For where jealousy and selfish ambition exist, there will be disorder and every vile practice. But the wisdom from above is first pure, then peaceable,

gentle, open to reason, full of mercy and good fruits, impartial and sincere. And a harvest of righteousness is sown in peace by those who make peace.
James 3:13-18

Guiding Questions

What person in the Bible, history, literature, or film needed wisdom?

When, why, and how should we (or should we NOT) be wise?

Vices
Wisdom can be a virtue in its best and most pure form, but it can quickly become a vice in its extreme form (disdain) or when it is lacking (ignorance). Continue contemplating wisdom by looking at these two misrepresentations of this virtue.

(+) Disdain
Definition: dislike of someone or something that you have determined is not worthy

A righteous man knows the rights of the poor; a wicked man does not understand such knowledge.
Proverbs 29:7

(-) Ignorance
Definition: lack of knowledge, understanding, or information about something

As obedient children, do not be conformed to the passions of your former ignorance.
I Peter 1:14

Guiding Questions

When have you experienced a person being disdainful or ignorant?

What situations cause you to be disdainful or ignorant?

When have you experienced wisdom from someone in your life?

How can you cultivate the virtue of wisdom in your life?

Circle a number to rate yourself in this virtue:

(-) ignorance			**Wisdom**			disdain (+)		
1	2	3	4	5	4	3	2	1

What kind of person do you want to be?

I am disdainful when...

I show ignorance when...

I show wisdom when...

I want to be...

Cultivating Virtue

Contemplation #60

(-) in deficiency	**VIRTUE**	(+) in excess
boorishness	**Wit**	buffoonery

"Wit, without wisdom, is salt without meat."
George Horne

WIT

Definition: the ability to see the humor in a situation and use words in an intelligent and amusing way

Comedians, court jesters, and fools often have the opportunity and ability to speak the truth to a leader or a society that others are too scared to say. Sometimes they are witty, but other times they are buffoons or boorish with their words and actions. Seeking to cultivate the virtue of wit can sometimes be difficult because there are so few good examples for us in modern society. Great books from authors such as Shakespeare and Twain often give us good examples of wit. Wit is smart, subtle, and clever without being rude, unkind, or malicious. Sarcastic comments toward a person are often quick and clever but lack the wisdom or sensitivity to strike the perfect balance to be witty.

Then Elijah said to the prophets of Baal, "Choose for yourselves one bull and prepare it first, for you are many, and call upon the name of your god, but put no fire to it." And they took the bull that was given them, and they prepared it and called upon the name of Baal from morning until noon, saying, "O Baal, answer us!" But there was no voice, and no one answered. And they limped around the altar that they

had made. And at noon Elijah mocked them, saying, "Cry aloud, for he is a god. Either he is musing, or he is relieving himself, or he is on a journey, or perhaps he is asleep and must be awakened."
I Kings 18:25-27

Guiding Questions

What person in the Bible, history, literature, or film needed to be witty?

When, why, and how should we (or should we NOT) be witty?

Vices

Wit can be a virtue in its best and most pure form, but it can quickly become a vice in its extreme form (buffoonery) or when it is lacking (boorishness). Continue contemplating wit by looking at these two misrepresentations of this virtue.

(+) Buffoonery

Definition: a person that does thoughtlessly silly things to make other people laugh

When I was a child, I spoke like a child, I thought like a child, I reasoned like a child. When I became a man, I gave up childish ways.
I Corinthians 13:11

(-) Boorishness

Definition: behaving rudely

Therefore encourage one another and build one another up, just as you are doing.
I Thessalonians 5:11

Guiding Questions

When have you experienced a person being a buffoon or boorish?

What situations cause you to be a buffoon or boorish?

When have you experienced wit from someone in your life?

How can you cultivate the virtue of wit in your life?

Circle a number to rate yourself in this virtue:

(-) boorishness				Wit		buffoonery (+)		
1	2	3	4	5	4	3	2	1

What kind of person do you want to be?

I am a buffoon when...

I am boorish when...

I am witty when...

I want to be...

CHAPTER III

Conclusion

So, what's next? Make it a habit to ask yourself, "What type of person do I want to be?" Revisit this list of virtues often and continue to contemplate and cultivate a deeper understanding of yourself and ways that you can be more like Christ. A list of virtues is a fantastic opportunity to practically focus on ways to mirror our Savior.

In the 1990s, there were wrist bands that read WWJD and symbolized "What Would Jesus Do?" You could answer the question in the following ways:

"Jesus would be _____ *fill in the virtue* ."
or
"Jesus would not be _____ *fill in the vice* ."

Again, this is not an exhaustive list of virtues, and Jesus is much more than just a moral guide or perfectly virtuous human. He is our LORD and Savior, and we have no hope to be good or develop in virtue apart from Him. If you are not already a Christian, pray to God and ask Him to save you. If you are a Christian, ask the Holy Spirit to guide you and convict you of ways you can be more virtuous.

Find a community such as a classical Christian school, church, small group study, or a few friends that want a flourishing life focused on living to the glory of God alone. May God bless you and keep you as you seek to live for Him!

REFERENCES

Aristotle., Bartlett, R. C., & Collins, S. D. (2011). *Aristotle's Nicomachean ethics.* Chicago: University of Chicago Press.

Aristotle's Ethics: Table of Virtues and Ethics. (2019). Retrieved December 22, 2019, from https://www.cwu.edu/~warren/Unit1/aristotles_virtues_and_vices.htm.

Awaken the Greatness Within. (2019). Retrieved August 15 - December 22, 2019, from https://www.awakenthegreatnesswithin.com.

Bible Gateway. (2019). Retrieved August 15 - December 22, 2019, from https://www.biblegateway.com.

Bible Study Tools. (2019). Retrieved August 15 - December 22, 2019, from https://www.biblestudytools.com.

Brainy Quote. (2019). Retrieved August 15 - December 22, 2019, from https://www.brainyquote.com.

Cambridge Dictionary. (2019). Retrieved August 15 - December 22, 2019, from https://dictionary.cambridge.org.

Crossway Bibles. (2007). *ESV: Study Bible: English standard version.* Wheaton, Ill: Crossway Bibles.

Open Bible. (2019). Retrieved August 15 - December 22, 2019, from https://www.openbible.info.

Quote Ambition. (2019). Retrieved August 15 - December 22, 2019, from http://www.quoteambition.com.

Merriam-Webster. (2019). Retrieved August 15 - December 22, 2019, from https://www.merriam-webster.com.

Thesaurus.com. (2019). Retrieved August 15 - December 22, 2019, from https://www.thesaurus.com.

Wise Old Sayings. (2019). Retrieved August 15 - December 22, 2019, from http://www.wiseoldsayings.com.

Word Hippo. (2019). Retrieved August 15 - December 22, 2019, from https://www.wordhippo.com.

Zondervan NIV study Bible. (2002). Barker, K. L. (Ed.). Rev. ed. Grand Rapids, MI: Zondervan.

ABOUT THE AUTHOR

 Dr. Timothy Dernlan is a speaker, consultant, author, and visionary Christian school leader. He is passionate about advancing Christian community and culture through education. He taught theater, math, rhetoric, physical education, personal finance, leadership, communication, and systematic theology before turning his focus to school leadership.

Much of his early life was influenced by the sport of wrestling. He won All-American honors while at Purdue University, represented the United States as an athlete at the Pan American Championships, and competed in the 2000 and 2004 final Olympic Trials. He coached at Purdue, Ohio State, Penn State, Lehigh, and Ashland University and was named the NCAA Midwest Region Coach of the Year in 2008.

Dr. Dernlan has served as principal, headmaster, head of school, and superintendent of Christian school systems ranging in size from 200 to 1300 students. Dernlan and his wife were married in 2000 and have four children.

MORE INFORMATION

For more information from Dr. Timothy Dernlan, please visit
www.TimDernlan.com

For more information on Classical Christian Education, visit
www.ClassicalChristianEducation.org

Made in the USA
Middletown, DE
10 September 2024